BAY WINDOW BOHEMIA

BAY WINDOW BOHEMIA

An Account of
the Brilliant Artistic World
of Gaslit San Francisco

Oscar Lewis

Preface by Kevin Starr

Yosemite-DiMaggio
618 Grand Avenue
Oakland, California 94610

Illustrations by courtesy of the Society of California Pioneers, San Francisco; The California Historical Society, San Francisco; and the Bancroft Library, University of California, Berkeley.

Cover art by Jim Kingwell

Printed in the United States
by
Braun-Brumfield, Inc., Ann Arbor, Michigan
ISBN 0-911819-01-0

PREFACE

Next month, Oscar Lewis will turn 90. Few men of letters based in the San Francisco Bay Area have enjoyed such a long and productive career. Mr. Lewis published his first magazine story in 1913 and has been busy ever since upon fourscore and more literary and historical projects of great importance to our understanding of the magnificent region, California, which has provided the premise and the context of most of Mr. Lewis' works. Many of Mr. Lewis' books have within his lifetime achieved the status of classics: *The Big Four* (1938), for instance, his narrative of the construction of the transcontinental railroad; *Silver Kings* (1947), the story of the Comstock Lode; and his remarkable novel, *I Remember Christine* (1942), which Lawrence Clark Powell correctly describes as the finest San Francisco novel since Frank Norris' *McTeague.*

My own personal favorite in the Oscar Lewis canon—a work now happily republished in this edition—is *Bay Window Bohemia,* first published in 1956. Like all of Mr. Lewis' books, *Bay Window Bohemia* is characterized by that special blend of solid research, graceful writing, and lively portraiture which pervades all of Mr. Lewis' work. Approaching his material with that catholicity of interest and generosity of response that characterized the true man of letters, Oscar Lewis digs deep into his subjects from the perspective of research, then

3

proceeds to transform the results of his investigation, not into pedantry, but into lively narratives in which important historical and literary arguments are advanced luminously and elegantly through the material itself. Oscar Lewis writes history with the exacting eye of the novelist and with a novelist's relish for the telling detail, the apt quote, the irony of event, and more subtly, the magic of the past.

Bay Window Bohemia shares honors with Franklin Walker's *San Francisco's Literary Frontier* (1939) for being the two finest literary narratives to deal with Bay Area letters. (Ella Sterling Cummins' *The Story of the Files,* published in 1893, runs a close third.) Indeed, *Bay Window Bohemia* takes up the story where Franklin Walker leaves it, at that moment when the literary frontier was over and a new generation, many of them California-born, were launching themselves into literary and artistic careers that would, in retrospect, make San Francisco of the *fin de siecle* shimmer with a brilliance equal to that (if not superior!) of the literary frontier.

Here within this relatively brief book—at once so economical and so lavish—Oscar Lewis has summoned forth and memorialized in narrative panorama the men and women who felt in gaslit San Francisco the full promise of Bohemia, life lived according to norms of pleasure and art. And here they are, each of them coming alive under Oscar Lewis' loving gaze, brought together, despite their many differences, in the crucible of *fin de siecle* San Francisco: Edward Robeson Taylor, the poet-attorney-physician called upon to serve as mayor of San Francisco; Willis Polk, then at the beginnings of his great career in architecture; Ambrose Bierce, surveying it all with lofty Olympian disdain; Gertrude Atherton, laying plans for her escape to Europe; Robert Louis Stevenson, pursuing his beloved to San Francisco and whose sojourn here provided the local community with a touchstone, a mood of reverie and remembrance that has lasted to this day; Douglas Tilden the sculptor; James D. Phelan the politician; Giuseppe Coppa, the restauranteur whose establishment provided the Bohemians with their home away from home (they decorated the walls of Coppa's with an astonishing series of murals); James J. (Gentleman Jim) Corbett, the Olympic Club boxing instructor destined to win the world's heavyweight championship; John O'Hara Cosgrove, the editor of the *Wave,* a magazine employing the talented likes of such aspiring writers as Frank Norris, and the Irwin brothers, Will and Wallace; Nora May French, beautiful, haunted, doomed; photographer Arnold Genthe; historians Hubert Howe Bancroft and Theodore H. Hittell; gardener John McLaren, busy about the creation of Golden Gate Park; educators David Starr Jordan and Joseph Le Conte . . . the rollcall of names of creative personalities finding their way into this book is endless. What Oscar Lewis has done in *Bay Window Bohemia* is to provide the first map, the preliminary guide, to this era of urban creativity. All future studies of San Francisco in this remarkable era must make their beginning with this book, in which the remembered—Frank Norris, Jack London, Robinson Jeffers, Maynard Dixon, Ambrose Bierce, Helena Modjeska—and cherished mainly in local memory —Dan O'Connell, Frank Pixley, Lily Hitchcock Coit, Charles Warren Stoddard—are given equal billing.

That, after all, is how outbursts of urban creativity truly happen—all of a piece, those destined for greatness working alongside those whose contribution is combined to the establishment of an ambience, a passing moment. In *Bay Window Bohemia,* Oscar Lewis celebrates one and all, whatever subsequent history has made of them, because all contributed in great or trivial ways to an energetic, fruitful, optimistic decade-plus in the history of San Francisco. This, for me, is part of the power of this book and why it deserves to be re-issued. *Bay Window Bohemia* encourages us not to lose faith in San Francisco or in cities in general. There is, this book suggests, a special affinity, a creative relationship. between urban culture and the arts that, despite all difficulties, manages to reassert itself at least every other generation. In the case of San Francisco, periods of creativity asserted themselves in the pre-railroad era, the *fin de siecle* which Oscar Lewis described, and the 1950s when two groups, the expatriate Beats and the indigenous poets, combined forces to achieve what Kenneth Rexroth correctly described as the San Francisco Literary Renaissance. Franklin Walker, as I say, has borne wonderful witness to this first period, and Oscar Lewis to its revival in the *fin de siecle.* Someday, perhaps, we will have an equally engaging narrative of the 1950s era. In the interim, *Bay Window Bohemia* sets standards for any such future work. In a very real sense, Mr. Oscar Lewis, as he reaches the venerable age of 90, is himself a survivor from the city he so lovingly describes. Like the San Francisco of that era, Oscar Lewis is learned, civilized, gracious, and above all else, animated by a persistent optimism based on a love of life and cities and creative expression.

Kevin Starr
18 April 1983
San Francisco

FOREWORD

On the pages that follow, an attempt has been made to tell something of the notable literary and artistic renaissance that took place in San Francisco during the closing years of the last century.

What, it might be asked, was there about the town that formed an environment so favorable to the development of talented youngsters in painting, writing, the drama, music, and indeed in virtually every form of art?

A number of theories have been advanced to explain the phenomenon. One is that the natural charm of the setting, plus the mild, stimulating climate, not only instilled in residents an awareness of the beauties of the physical world about them, but aroused in many an urge to capture something of these qualities in poetry and prose, in painting, music, and drama.

There are, too, those who have maintained that the inspiration came not from such sources, but from the extraordinarily diverse nature of the city's residents, in whose veins flowed the blood of adventurous forebears drawn to those shores from every corner of the world by the lure of the gold discoveries a generation earlier.

Foreword

Yet another theory is that the town's artistic fruitfulness during the decade of the 1890s was the direct result of certain features of community life that had existed there since pioneer times; namely, that the forty-niners, cut off by thousands of miles from the older centers of culture, were forced either to provide their own diversions, their own art and literature and drama, or do without.

Whichever of these hypotheses is correct—or if, as seems likely, each might have contributed its share—the fact remains that during the closing years of the last century the town saw the emergence of a large and uncommonly able group of workers in the arts: poets, novelists, painters, cartoonists, sculptors, musicians, actors, and journalists.

It saw, too, a lively interest in these matters on the part of the populace as a whole; an interest—and appreciation—that was expressed by their purchase of the works of local painters and sculptors and, in the fields of music and the drama, by their liberal patronage of the town's many theaters, concert halls, and other places of entertainment.

That the San Francisco of the 1890s had qualities that set it apart from other American cities was generally acknowledged, not alone by visitors from elsewhere but by the residents themselves. As evidence of this, both strangers and old-timers pointed out that, unlike the staid decorum of most Anglo-Saxon communities, San Francisco had an air of lighthearted gaiety, its fun-loving inhabitants ever ready to put aside dull business concerns and join in having a good time.

Because of that characteristic on the part of virtually every San Franciscan, the facilities for recreation and amusement were uncommonly varied. These ranged from a multiplicity of corner barrooms in every part of the city, on through beer gardens, amusement parks, and picnic grounds, to theaters

8

and restaurants of a number and quality out of all proportion to the community's size.

While this spirit of lightheartedness manifested itself to a considerable degree among all sections of the population, it was particularly evident in those who made up the town's extensive artistic colony. For they, like their Bohemian brethren of every age and clime, lived in a closely knit world of their own, consciously apart from what they chose to regard as the dull pursuits of their moneygrubbing neighbors.

Thus drawn together by mutual interests and prejudices— and by the spur of economic necessity—they tended to congregate in one particular quarter of the city, a district of outmoded brick and wooden buildings put up in the early 1850s, where rents were low and an abundance of cheap but passably good restaurants, mostly French and Italian, lay close at hand.

In such congenial surroundings, and in the company of others of like tastes and ambitions, there lived and worked throughout the 1890s as picturesque—and talented—a group of artists, sculptors, actors, musicians, and writers as existed anywhere in the country. Not all those who served their apprenticeship in that environment became well-known figures in the world of arts and letters, although a surprisingly large number of them did.

Those whose names are recalled today were for the most part men and women who, having established local reputations, pushed on to New York, where, then as now, were concentrated the major publishing houses, the leading magazines and art dealers, and the foremost theatrical producers and booking agents. On the other hand, there were many who, spurning the allurements of the East Coast, chose to remain year after year in their big, high-ceilinged rooms fronting on Washington, Jackson, and Montgomery streets, living a hand-

9

to-mouth existence yet keeping alive the traditions established during the brief but fruitful heyday of the quarter.

On the following pages something will be told of the numerous groups who lived and worked and played in *fin de siècle* San Francisco, of the studios and bars and restaurants where they foregathered, of their youthful exuberance and scorn of conventions, of their hoaxes and pranks and good-natured deviltry, and, above all, of the record of solid accomplishment they left behind to sustain and enrich the cultural heritage of the city.

In assembling the material here presented, one of the author's main reliances has been on the recollections of those old-timers—their number growing less each year—whose memories go back to the turn of the century and before; on the written memoirs, both published and in manuscript, of participants; on certain collections of letters and personal memorabilia now in private or public hands, and on the files of the town's daily and weekly journals covering the period from the later 1880s until the era came to a final, jolting end on the morning of April 18, 1906.

The author gratefully acknowledges the interest, generosity, and unfailing helpfulness of those individuals and organizations that have made possible this salute to the blithesome, carefree "City That Was."

Oscar Lewis

CONTENTS

Illustrations facing page 126

BAY WINDOW BOHEMIA

CHAPTER 1

The Setting

I.

As San Francisco entered the 1890s, rounding out the first half century of its existence, it was by no means unaware of its position as the West Coast metropolis, the business, financial, and cultural center of a region that embraced a full third of the nation's area. When that decade opened, the town's helter-skelter beginnings seemed far in the past, and the residents one and all took pride in the fine modern city that had arisen on the site of the old.

Nor did they boast only of the signs of material growth and progress that were everywhere visible: the rows of three-, four-, and five-story buildings that lined the downtown streets; the big, ornate wooden mansions that had gone up on Nob Hill and the newly opened Western Addition; the block after block of close-packed cottages—each with its sun-catching bay window in front—spreading over the sandhills in every direction, or the chimneys of new factories adding to the pall of smoke that hung over the industrial area to the south of Market.

These evidences of progress were gratifying to be sure, but many San Franciscans of the day were concerned, too, with other aspects of their town's coming of age. Growth and material prosperity were well enough, but in their view these were incidentals. What mainly interested them was the community's emergence as a literary and artistic center, as the spot above all others in the West that offered an environment favorable to the cultivation of the genteel arts: painting, music, and drama, and—at least equally important—their collateral pleasures of eating and drinking.

It was, of course, a period when interest in such matters was on the increase all over the country, but nowhere was it more widespread or deeply felt than in San Francisco. For despite their remoteness from the old established artistic centers—or perhaps because of it—the town's aesthetes prided themselves on keeping in touch with every phase of the artistic and literary revolution that was yearly growing more manifest as the century neared its close.

Since its beginnings, San Francisco had never been content with half measures, and now, proud of its position as the West's leading citadel of culture, nothing would do but that it must be in the forefront of the movement. Toward the mid-1890s its newspapers somewhat self-consciously blossomed out with a new phrase: *fin de siècle*. Their society columns carried accounts of *fin de siècle* receptions, cotillions, and other social functions; *fin de siècle* hats and shoes and manteaux were featured in their advertisements, and the term was presently being applied to about every type of merchandise offered the public, from parlor and bedroom suites of carved walnut to the latest works of such "advanced" novelists as George du Maurier and Mrs. Humphry Ward.

But for all this new-found sophistication, this eagerness to embrace whatever was the *dernier cri* in art, in dress, or in behavior, life somehow went on in much the same manner as it had during the humdrum 1870s and 1880s. The modish parlors of the day were carpeted from wall to wall with brightly figured body Brussels, and on their walls were huge steel engravings of Biblical scenes, the two favorites being The Return of the Prodigal Son and The Feast of Belshazzar. At the organ or square piano the young ladies of the house entertained callers with Leybach's "Fifth Nocturne" or "The Maiden's Prayer," and if asked for something a bit more lively, obliged with "The Stub-Toe Polka." To be sure, at young people's parties the bars were let down and guests and hostesses went through their repertory of currently popular songs, both comic and sentimental, their prime favorites being "Champagne Charley Is My Name," "Tommy, Make Room for Your Uncle," "The Virginia Rosebud," and "There's a Letter in the Candle."

At such gatherings one musical novelty that never failed to charm listeners was a rendering of "Poor Whippoorwill," with one young lady playing the accompaniment in the parlor while her fellow artiste stood outside in the hall as she sang, the door connecting the two chambers being closed. Other polite diversions within the domestic circle were looking at the family albums or admiring the lifelike objects visible through the newfangled stereopticons. On that instrument views of historic spots both at home and abroad were preferred, for these were not only entertaining but obviously had an educational value as well.

There was, to be sure, another side to the picture. For San Francisco was a seaport and, along with the sedate diversions of the scions of its leading families, it offered ample facilities for recreation of another sort. Sailors in from months-long cruises in the windjammers of the day—and newly paid off— found no lack of companions anxious to relieve them of the gold coins jangling in their pockets. As their ships docked they were met at the pierside by affable runners eager to pilot them to any number of snug harbors: waterfront rooming houses and dives and clip joints, brightly lit bars and gaming rooms, variety shows of the sort they wanted to see, and temples of love whose inmates were guaranteed to be the acme of amiability and pulchritude.

Most newly arrived seamen made straight for the Barbary Coast. Since the early 1850s the Coast had centered on lower Pacific Street and its adjacent alleys, but in the four decades that followed it had spread to the south and west, to and beyond the edges of Chinatown and Portsmouth Plaza. It was a region of closely built brick and wooden houses fronting on narrow streets and passageways that, all but deserted during the daylight hours, were filled from curb to curb every night of the year.

By the opening of the 1890s the area had been divided into several more or less distinct districts. The block on Pacific between Montgomery and Kearny was given over to a succession of hurdy-gurdy houses offering a variety of diversions to entertainment-starved sailors and visitors from the back country. These resorts were laid out in much the same manner as the sedate beer gardens farther uptown, with closely packed tables occupying the main floor and balcony, a bar extending the length of one wall, and, at the far end, a stage on which the entertainers—hoochy-koochy dancers, comedians, an occasional singer of sentimental ballads, and, invariably, a bevy of buxom chorus ladies—appeared at frequent intervals throughout the night.

Most such resorts had, too, a cleared space on which patrons danced, to the accompaniment of four- or six-piece orchestras, with one or another of a group of hostesses, it being a house rule that on returning to his table or the bar

18

the visitor must treat his partner to a drink of her choice. The fact that the lady invariably chose a bottle of what passed for champagne—the price of which ranged from five dollars upward, depending on the customer's resources or the degree of his sobriety—was his bad luck; if he protested too noisily, there were always bouncers on hand to toss him out on the sidewalk.

During its heyday this block-long cluster of deadfalls contributed some colorful words to the language. One was "hoodlum," first applied to gangs of thugs who infested the district during the early days; the word is thought to have been a corruption of their shout of "Huddle 'em" as they closed in on their victims. Another was the verb "to shanghai," that knavish art having been widely practiced in the dives of the Coast since the earliest days. The term had its origin in the fact that when the drugged seaman awoke he was likely to find himself outward bound on a months-long voyage to that Chinese port.

The Coast had the distinction, too, of originating a number of dances that, during the late 1890s and early 1900s, made their way into the ballrooms of the country, largely displacing the time-honored waltzes, polkas, and schottisches. One such was the "turkey trot," first danced at Purcell's widely patronized Pacific Street resort. Another was the "Texas tommy," the Thalia's contribution toward the emancipation of the nation's younger and more agile dancers from the staid steps fancied by their elders.

While prostitutes were by no means unknown, or unwelcome, at the "Terrific Street" resorts—several had upper floors divided into rooms to which hostesses might pilot customers—this was looked on as a minor source of revenue, the main profits coming from the sale of drinks at the tables and bar. The main red-light districts were located elsewhere: in the area that lay between Clay, Kearny, Pacific, and Dupont streets; along the edges of Chinatown as far as Bush Street; and, farther uptown, on both sides of Dupont from Market to Post, with an offshoot extending the length of an intersecting alley called Morton Street.

The houses that operated in these districts each sheltered a different sort of inmate and in the main catered to a different clientele. In the area to the south and west of Portsmouth Plaza the streets and alleys were solidly lined with cribs, some flaunting red lights above their entrances, others advertising their wares by means of groups of girls sitting in the windows of their ground-floor parlors.

This was the district most frequented by the hoi polloi: sailors and dockworkers from the waterfront, ranchers and miners and lumberjacks in town for a fling, and such locals as preferred the variegated assemblage of races represented there to the more specialized—and expensive—types to be found elsewhere. Here the industry was conducted at its baldest, most matter-of-fact level, in surroundings that were barren, sordid, and completely lacking the trappings of pseudo romance.

A block or two farther to the south and west, centering on Waverly Place and Sullivan Alley, were a group of parlor houses operated and staffed by Chinese. Some of these were elaborately fitted up in the Oriental manner, with teakwood furniture and screens, embroidered hangings on their walls, and the rooms permeated with a cloyingly sweet aroma from incense pots that were kept burning during business hours. These catered both to whites and to the merchants, importers, and other prosperous members of the local Chinese colony. The inmates—"slave girls" they were termed by the clergy and press—had from the beginning been brought over for that purpose from the homeland, openly in the earlier years,

and later, their importation having been prohibited by law,
by smuggling them in, either directly from ships in the harbor
or across the Mexican or Canadian borders.)

(Throughout the length of Waverly Place—dubbed "The
Street of the Slaves" by the newspapers—the girls sat in tiny
cubicles, dressed in silks with an abundance of gold and jade
ornaments framing their thickly painted faces, while the
customers filed past, pausing before each cell and submitting
its occupant to a close scrutiny. In the more select houses the
inmates were invariably very young—some, it is said, no
more than twelve or thirteen—and their period of usefulness
was likewise brief, rarely extending more than five years. At
the end of that time they were either sent to one of the lowly
cribs on Bartlett or Brooklyn alleys or, if they were lucky,
taken as consort by one of their countrymen.)

During most of the 1890s the third major center of whore-
dom was half a dozen blocks farther to the south, in the midst
of the retail shopping district and cheek and jowl with the
town's most fashionable stores and promenades. Lining both
sides of Dupont Street (now Grant Avenue) from its junction
with Market to beyond Geary were a cluster of houses quite
different from the resorts of the Barbary Coast and Chinatown. These occupied a group of ornate wooden residences
put up in Civil War days, their former owners having moved
to one or another of the newer districts farther out.

In these prim establishments decorum and gentility were
the watchwords, with the madams exercising much care in the
selection of girls and quick to suppress any unseemly conduct on the part of the guests. Prices were substantially
higher at these genteel resorts but, so it was claimed, so
likewise was the type of entertainment provided. The inmates were not only young and amiable but were reputed to
be of a type superior to that of their less fortunate sisters

elsewhere in town. In fact, it was said to be the hope of every ambitious girl in the bagnios of the Coast and Bartlett Alley to "graduate" to one of the select Dupont Street resorts.

However, not all the houses in the downtown tenderloin, as it came to be called, were of this superior type. Crossing Dupont Street on the block between Geary and Post and extending from Kearny to Stockton is the narrow thoroughfare now called Maiden Lane but which in the 1890s was known as Morton Street and in some quarters as "Iodoform Alley." Here was an assemblage of resorts as varied—and depraved—as any in the city. Not only did it shelter harlots of all nations—including French, Chinese, Negroes, Mexicans, and Americans—but it was the hangout, too, of pickpockets, dope peddlers, and thugs of every description.

Although Morton Street, as stated, cut across the very center of the retail shopping district, it was scrupulously avoided by the town's respectable women, for to set foot within its confines was considered a serious breach of decorum. To guard against that possibility there was usually a policeman stationed at each end of the street charged with warning away the curious.

When, shortly after the turn of the century, the wily Abe Reuf made himself political boss of the town, he ordered a clean-up campaign during which every Morton Street resort was closed and padlocked. Moreover, unlike most such campaigns—which usually lasted only a week or two—this one remained in force for month after month. Meantime the property owners, one by one, got discouraged and sold out, the buyer in each case being an agent for the same Reuf. Then, having picked up nearly all the houses at bargain prices, he lifted the embargo and the street was presently again going full blast. It continued to boom until the entire area was laid waste by the fire of 1906. Today the former

Morton Street is a thoroughfare given over to gift shops, tearooms, cocktail bars, and the like, all of unimpeachable respectability.)

II.

Throughout the closing years of the century many changes took place in the physical aspect of the town. While the depression years of 1892–93 brought a general slowing down of activity, accompanied by many business failures and widespread unemployment, the effect soon passed and for the balance of the decade the town forged ahead at a steadily accelerating rate.

During these years two external events added substantially to its material prosperity. The first was the discovery of reputedly rich gold fields in the Klondike in 1896, which throughout the next two years drew thousands to the far north, many of whom outfitted themselves in San Francisco. Then, in 1898, came the outbreak of the Spanish-American War, during the course of which a steady stream of men and materials flowed through the port bound for the Philippines.

Stimulated by these and other factors, the town grew and prospered, its population rising from 298,997 in 1890 to 342,782 ten years later. Meantime row after row of bay-windowed dwellings were spreading over the sandhills beyond Van Ness Avenue, in the Mission District, and toward Twin Peaks, and in the business center scores of modest brick and wooden structures put up in the 1850s and 1860s were being torn down and replaced by buildings more in keeping with the city's new estate.

Thus in the summer of 1890 the *Chronicle* moved into its new red brick building at the corner of Market and Kearny streets. This was the city's first steel-frame structure and its ten stories, surmounted by a clock tower, dominated the downtown area. But not for long, for early fears that the skyscrapers then going up throughout the East were dangerous in this region where earthquakes were frequent were presently proved groundless and a number of other multiple-story buildings followed. The most impressive of these was that of sugar magnate Claus Spreckels, who in 1895 erected, on a site diagonally across Market Street from the *Chronicle's* new home, a nineteen-story tower in which to house his newspaper, the *Morning Call.*

There were numerous other new business blocks to which the residents could point with pride. In 1891 banker Darius Ogden Mills put up on the corner of Bush and Montgomery streets—long the site of Pratt's Hall, where many stirring early-day events had taken place—a handsome, ten-story office building named for its owner. This was followed by the eight-story brick and granite home of the Wells, Fargo Bank on the Market-Montgomery gore; by the Crocker Building on the adjacent triangular lot facing Market and Post streets; and as the decade neared its close, by half a dozen other structures that further changed the downtown skyline. In 1896 work was begun on the 662-foot-long Ferry Building at the foot of Market, the central tower of which—modeled on the Giralda Tower of the cathedral at Seville—has ever since stood as a sort of unofficial symbol of the city.

Nor was the building boom of the 1890s all confined to the business district. In the region to the west, which during the previous two decades had seen the rise of hundreds of ornate wooden residences, a variety of even more pretentious structures was put up: churches, schools, hospitals, and, along Washington Street, Pacific Avenue, and Broadway— where they commanded sweeping views of the bay—a score of impressive stone and brick residences, the homes of the Floods, Phelans, Irwins, Hellmans, and others of the town's bankers, merchants, transportation kings, or wealthy mine, lumber, and cattle owners.

The period saw, too, work continuing on the City Hall, which, as the 1890s opened, had already been under construction for the better part of two decades. Occupying a site at McAllister and Larkin streets which had been a cemetery in early days, it had progressed so slowly that by the time the 1890s rolled around local wits were referring to it as the "new City Hall ruins." The reason for that extremely leisurely rate of progress was twofold. First, the original plans— prepared by an architect who had won renown for his design of the New York state capitol at Albany—were on a scale that, as the San Francisco newspapers of the day triumphantly announced, would make it "the handsomest and most imposing municipal building in the nation." Second, the citizens, rejecting a proposal that its construction be financed by means of a bond issue—thereby spreading its cost over a generation or longer—voted instead to build it on a pay-as-you-go basis, a certain small percentage of the tax revenue being assigned to that purpose each year.

The result was that building would go on only so long as the current appropriation lasted—usually a matter of three or four months—whereupon all activity ceased until the next year's funds became available. By that piecemeal method costs skyrocketed. By the mid-1890s, $7,000,000 had been expended—more than six times the original estimate—and the job was still far from finished. Small wonder that the project became a standing joke with San Franciscans throughout the final years of the century, references to it by vaudeville comedians rarely failing to bring forth a wry laugh from their audiences.

III.

For many years prior to 1906, San Francisco shared with New Orleans the reputation of being the gayest city of the nation. There were few residents, even among those who most deplored that aspect of its life, who disagreed. These well knew that the activities and attitudes that had won it renown as "the Paris of America" had nothing to do with those phases of their city in which they took a proper pride: the beauty of its setting, its cosmopolitanism, the lighthearted gaiety with which the inhabitants went about their work and play; most of all its love of music, drama, and the other arts, and its benign attitude toward workers in these fields.

No, the town's fame—or, more accurately, its notoriety—elsewhere in the country was based on other aspects of communal life: its large and flourishing red-light districts, its wide-open gambling resorts, its waterfront dives and Barbary Coast deadfalls, and—not the least—its group of French restaurants, each with its upper floor divided into booths and in each booth a couch along one wall and a lock on its door with the key inside.

That their town was neither strait-laced nor puritanical all San Franciscans freely admitted—it would have been futile to argue to the contrary—but that it was a sink of iniquity, a modern Sodom or Gomorrah, they indignantly denied. True, it offered ample facilities by which those so inclined might indulge their gross or lusty appetites, but in that respect it was no different from scores of other seaport towns from Callao to Port Said.

But balancing that was another side of their city's cosmopolitanism; namely, its tolerance and sophistication, its engaging freedom from cant or hypocrisy. And, so its defenders stoutly maintained, it was because of those very qualities that life there took on a zest and sparkle unknown in more conventional communities, that its residents were encouraged to throw off their inhibitions and enjoy themselves to the full. More, it was a moral and intellectual climate that fostered an appreciation of those sensual pleasures that make for gracious living: good food and drink, good music and drama and other civilized pleasures, and, moreover, that created a highly congenial atmosphere for workers in the arts.

Residents were not at all inclined to argue with those who likened their city to Paris. Many, however, were at pains to make it clear that what their town most sought to emulate was not the vices of the French capital but its hospitality to art and literature, its flair for the best in food and drink and other adjuncts to full and gracious living, and the gaiety and zest for life of its people.

Some of those who wrote of the city during that period caught that attitude on the part of the populace, but by no means all of them. Numerous persons, both residents and visitors, recorded their impressions of the prefire town, and the conclusions reached were as many—and as different—as those who expressed them.

Thus, twenty-four-year-old Rudyard Kipling, spending a few days there in the spring of 1889, pronounced it "a mad city, inhabited by perfectly insane people whose women are of a remarkable beauty." Landing from the *City of Peking* after a tedious crossing of the Pacific, the youth, fresh from colonial India, found himself "tangled . . . in a hopeless maze of small wooden houses, dust, street-refuse, and children who play with empty kerosene tins . . ." Having made his way to the Palace Hotel—then the city's pride—he stubbornly refused to be impressed, dismissing it as "a seven-storied

27

warren of humanity with a thousand rooms in it," the most conspicuous feature of which was, to his mind, the great brass cuspidors displayed—and frequently used—not only in the downstairs lobby and bar but on the stairs and in the bedrooms, "yea, and in chambers even more sacred than these"— whatever he meant by that.

Hardly anywhere in the town did the bespectacled youth find anything of which to approve. The hotel clerk revealed himself as a boor, and inattentive to the wants of arriving guests; the natives, who imagined themselves to be talking English, in reality "spoke the language of thieves," while to venture out on the streets was to be set upon by a swarm of confidence men and cardsharpers and, as like as not, to witness a murder or two. Only the women, "of generous build, large, well-groomed, and attired in raiment that even to my inexperienced eyes must have cost much," won his unqualified approval; these he found "very fair."

Kipling, however, was not alone in such opinions. Another well-known literary figure, Gertrude Atherton, herself a native daughter, on returning in the mid-1890s after several years in Europe, found as little to admire as had the young Briton. "I used," she later recalled, "to walk past those long rows of houses, drab, with bow-windows, as alike as a row of lead pencils in a box, visualizing the dull, eventless lives of those who lived in them, depressing my spirits to zero . . . I doubted if anywhere on earth could one feel so isolated, so blue, so stranded, as in San Francisco. Well had it been called the Jumping-Off Place. In the nineties, despite the sentimentalists, it was gray and ugly and depressing."

There was, of course, a brighter side to the shield. Robert Louis Stevenson, who spent some months in and about the city in the late 1870s, being then unknown and ill, and a briefer period a dozen years later after world-wide success

28

had come to him, found much to admire, not only in its bracing climate and carefree people but in the beauty of its setting. Of the town's cosmopolitanism he had Loudon Dodd, a character in *The Wrecker*, state: "She is . . . the most interesting city in the Union, and the hugest smelting-pot of races and precious metals . . ." Dodd spoke particularly of Little Italy, where he had spent much time gazing "in at the windows of small eating-shops transported bodily from Genoa or Naples, with their macaroni, and chianti flasks and portraits of Garibaldi," and of Little Mexico close by, "with its crazy wooden houses and endless crazy wooden stairs and perilous mountain goat paths in the sand." Chinatown, too, was one of Dodd's—and Stevenson's—favorite haunts, and North Beach, and the slums south of Market. "Nor did I even neglect Nob Hill, which is itself a kind of slum, being the habitat of the mere millionaire."

One of the most eloquent of many paeans in praise of the town was Will Irwin's *The City That Was*, first published in the New York *Sun* on April 21, 1906, while the fire, kindled by the earthquake three days earlier, still raged. Irwin, who, following his graduation from Stanford, had worked on local newspapers before moving on to New York, began his tribute to the old town with this quotation from another San Franciscan marooned on the East Coast, the lightweight prize fighter Jimmie Britt: "I'd rather be a busted lamp post on Battery Street . . . than the Waldorf-Astoria."

Prefire San Francisco was, stated Irwin, "the gayest, lightest hearted, most pleasure loving city on the western continent, and in many ways the most interesting and romantic." While granting that it "presented at first sight a disreputable appearance"—mainly the result of much "atrocious architecture" perpetrated during the 1870s and 1880s—he dwelt nostalgically with many aspects of the old town: its spectacular setting, its invigorating, heat-repelling summer fogs, its streets and docks and teeming foreign quarters; most of all with the high spirits and abounding zest of life exhibited by all classes, from the humblest to the most exalted.

Like young Kipling a quarter century earlier, Irwin did not neglect to pay tribute to the pulchritude and great vitality of the town's women. "The mixed stock," wrote he, "has given her that regularity of features which goes with a blend of bloods; the climate has perfected and rounded her figure, out-of-door exercise from earliest youth has given her a deep bosom; the cosmetic mists have made her complexion soft and brilliant." He went on to quote pridefully the fact that "at the University of California, where the student body is nearly all native, the gymnasium measurements show that the girls are a little more than two inches taller than their sisters at Vassar and Michigan." His all-inclusive requiem ended thus: "The bonny, merry city—the good, gray city—O that one who mingled the wine of her abounding life with the wine of his youth should live to write the obituary of Old San Francisco!"

The catastrophe of 1906 called forth yet another eloquent tribute to the prefire town, this one from the hands of William Marion Reedy, editor and publisher of a then widely read St. Louis weekly, *Reedy's Mirror*. "Life was lived in Frisco," wrote he. "It was a little of Paris, of Rome, of Pekin. It was a town of temperament in which lightness blent with a native beauty sense . . . Its people loved it with the intensity with which we love what we are likely to lose." Having set forth those characteristics that had gained it a unique place among American cities—its cosmopolitanism, its tolerance, its magnanimity toward workers in the arts and letters, and, above all, the spirit of joyousness that animated the citizenry in their festive moods—Reedy concluded with these words:

The Setting

"Vale et Ave Frisco the beautiful, the glad, the strong, the stricken, the invincible. Down with her went our hearts. Up with her go our souls. The country's hope and faith and love are more fired than the shuddering earth and all these are in the tear brightened eyes of Frisco looking out from the wreck over the Pacific where lies the future big with mighty fates for her beyond prophecy."

When copies of the *Mirror* containing this tribute reached the wrecked town, they were passed from hand to hand and literally read to rags. It was widely proclaimed the finest and most understanding eulogy ever accorded the city—and all this despite the fact that when the author wrote his panegyric he had never laid eyes on the place. It was, in fact, not until some fourteen years later, during the Democratic National Convention of 1920, that he paid his first visit to San Francisco, and it was there, curiously—and some say fittingly—enough, that he was taken ill and died.

CHAPTER 2

"A Little of Paris, of Rome, of Pekin"

I.

In the early 1900s young Frank Norris, in a little volume of essays entitled *The Responsibilities of the Novelist*, pronounced San Francisco one of the few authentic "story cities" of the nation, and went on to state that life there possessed a variety and sparkle that proved an unfailing source of inspiration to writers of fiction. It was, he maintained, one of but three such cities in the country, the other two being New Orleans and New York. By way of driving home his point, he wrote: "Fancy a novel about Chicago or Buffalo, let us say, or Nashville, Tennessee!" A year or two later O. Henry, having quoted Norris's pronouncement, accepted the challenge and penned a dramatic yarn with Nashville as its locale, at the end of which he inquired ironically: "I wonder what's doing in Buffalo?"

Notwithstanding this rebuttal, there was much to be said for Norris's original contention. Prefire San Francisco was indeed a town that, to one who had eyes to see, was possessed of endless color and romance. Those visiting it for the first time were struck by a certain gaiety on the faces of those who day and night thronged the downtown promenades; it was, stated one newcomer, as though a spirit of carnival pervaded the city from one year's end to the next. As a matter of fact, such was its cosmopolitanism that there was scarcely a time when the members of one or another racial group were not congregating to observe either some religious festival or national holiday of their homeland. Such festive gatherings, frequent throughout the year, were especially numerous during the summer and fall, when rarely a day passed without one or more being held somewhere in the town.

These ranged from assemblages at which those of common ancestry and traditions—French, Irish, Scandinavian, Italian, Japanese, or any one of a dozen others—congregated to commemorate some traditional event, meeting in their own church or hall or at the home of one of their number. These were in the main gatherings of special groups, in which the residents as a whole had no part. On the other hand, there were certain such festivities that took on the aspect of city-wide holidays.

In the latter class by far the most colorful—and noisy—was Tong Yan Sun Neen, known to the Occidental heathens as Chinese New Year, which annually took place in late January or early February. Then for a period of seven days a carnival spirit held sway throughout Chinatown, during which its entire population, augmented by thousands of countrymen from far and near, jammed its narrow streets and alleys while the whole central part of the city echoed day and night with a continuous roar.

The source of the noise was of course firecrackers, prodigious numbers of which were set off during the week-long celebrations, their avowed purpose being to scare off any evil spirits that might be hovering about bent on spoiling the fun.

34

It was a period of rejoicing and good will, when bills were paid, gifts exchanged, and the residents, decked out in their most festive costumes, exchanged ceremonious calls. Some of the outfits—those of prosperous merchants and their women and progeny—were extraordinarily colorful: rich silks resplendent with embroideries and gold ornaments set off with jade and semiprecious stones.

The high point of the week came on the final day, when the Lion—a resplendent dragon symbolizing good luck—was paraded through the streets, its head pausing at each doorway to receive gifts set out for it, and its long, undulating body, supported by scores of celebrants, trailing along behind. This, by common consent, was the climactic event in which the entire city joined, with throngs converging on Dupont and its intersecting streets to admire the displays of art objects in the shop windows and buy the delicacies—lichee nuts, melon seeds, ginger, candied coconut, citron, and orange peel —offered on the sidewalk stands.

Tong Yan Sun Neen was the period, too, when the town's Chinese servants—and few were the households that did not have at least one as cook, houseboy, or general factotum— returned bearing gifts for members of the family: a pot of Chinese lilies or a packet of tea for the mistress, bags of nuts or candied melon rind or bright red firecrackers for the children, a scroll or box or quaint desk ornament for the master of the house.

From the beginning Chinatown had proved a prolific source of copy to local writers. It was not, however, until the early 1890s that there appeared on the scene one who wrote of the district with real understanding and appreciation of the manner of life lived there; namely, Chester Bailey Fernald. Born in Boston in 1869, Fernald reached San Francisco while still in his early twenties, worked for several years as a draughtsman, then went into newspaper work, at the same time contributing stories and sketches to the magazine section of the Sunday *Chronicle*. In 1893 that paper sent him to Washington, D.C., as a political correspondent, and he subsequently traveled extensively: to Alaska, the Orient, and Europe. In 1898 he settled in England and lived there—with frequent jaunts to other parts of the world—until his death, at the age of sixty-nine, in 1938.

Although Fernald's stay in San Francisco was comparatively brief, he yet made one permanent contribution to the literature of the city. Like many another newcomer, the youth was captivated by the variety and color and smells and squalor of the quarter, and he took to haunting its streets and alleys, observing the behavior of its denizens with a keen and appreciative eye. Presently he began putting his impressions on paper, producing a series of sketches that were not slow in attracting the attention of discriminating readers. For these bore little resemblance to the usual outsider's view of Chinatown, which ordinarily treated it as a bizarre and mysterious quarter, romantic perhaps, but with the lives of its inhabitants having little in common with those of their Caucasian neighbors.

In his sketches—many of them cast in the form of fiction—Fernald was little concerned with such surface manifestations. Instead he sought to cast light on the day-by-day concerns of its residents, their business and domestic relationships, and something of their philosophy of life. All this was told from so sympathetic a viewpoint, and so amiably set forth the virtues and foibles of the race, that it did much to soften the San Franciscan's deep-seated prejudices against the Orientals, who for many years had been looked on as crafty, scheming heathens and the source of most of the city's economic and financial woes.

"A Little of Paris, of Rome, of Pekin"

In 1895, Fernald's Chinatown sketches were gathered up by a local publisher and issued in a little book called *The Cat and the Cherub*, now long out of print and difficult to come by. Its title is taken from one of the stories in the volume, a tale of five-year-old Hoo Chee, son of a prosperous ginseng merchant. An outline of this yarn will reveal something of the author's simple themes and his engaging, half-whimsical manner of presenting them. One day Hoo Chee slips away from his home, carrying his pet cat, One-Two, in his arms, and follows a young American art student, Bayley Arenam—whom he has long admired—to her house.

Invited inside by Miss Arenam—who proceeds to model the child's head in clay—Hoo Chee and his cat spend a happy afternoon and evening, being made much of by the girl and her friends. Meantime little Hoo Chee has been missed at home, and his father, fearing that he has been kidnaped and is being held for ransom by a rival tong, craftily offers a reward—not for the boy but for the cat. In the end the Arenams' Chinese servant learns the child's identity and, having collected the reward, restores Hoo Chee and One-Two safely to the paternal roof. A simple tale, but told with so warm an appreciation of the human factors involved as to give many local readers a new insight into the inner lives of the despised "Chinks."

Another of Fernald's stories, "The Gentleman in the Barrel," is in a quite different vein, being an account of how a local herb doctor, one Wing Shee, temporarily down on his luck and about to be evicted from his garret room on Beverly Place, undertakes—for a fee of $300—to secure for the heads of one of the tongs the names of members of a rival tong, which are engrossed on the walls of its closely guarded headquarters. This second tong was known as the Ho Wang Company, and before the world it represented itself as a reputable dealer in wine, its inner chamber having ranged about its walls a number of big oak casks.

To gain entrance, the crafty Wing Shee procures a similar cask, stows himself and certain of his belongings inside, and has an expressman friend, one Snubby Taggerty, deliver him to the rooms of the Ho Wang Company. Some eighteen hours later the faithful Taggerty, having recovered the barrel from under the eyes of two guards, lugs it back to the Beverly Place garret, releases its badly cramped occupant, and looks on approvingly as Wing Shee turns over the three hundred names he has copied from its walls and collects his fee.

After his employers have gone, Wing Shee confesses to his expressman friend that the names he has taken down are those not of present members of the Ho Wang Company, but of deceased ex-members; moreover, that during his confinement he has learned the real business in which the company is engaged. This is none other than a scheme by which each member brings a supply of gold coins to the nightly meetings; these are placed in barrels, carefully measured amounts of water and sand are added, and the whole rolled vigorously back and forth for several hours. During that process substantial amounts of gold are "sweated" from the coins; these are recovered, divided among the members, and the coins put back in circulation.

Taggerty presently leaves to turn in the names of the gold-sweaters to the authorities and gain for himself and Wing Shee the standing reward offered for such information. Thereupon, the doctor, who during his stay in the barrel had whiled away the hours by reading the esoteric literature of his homeland, takes up his quaint little stringed instrument, lights his opium pipe, and, lying at ease on his pallet, muses thus:

"The best of it . . . is that, after twenty years, I have at last finished the 'Story of How Yuen Liu Taught the Stork to

Play Shuttle-Cock,' which, to me, is the most stupid and impossible of the Seven Thousand Classics."

In his later years Fernald wrote much for the theater. One of the most successful of his plays was *The Cat and the Cherub*, based on his earlier short story. This was presently made into an opera, *L'Oracolo*, by Franco Leoni, which was long a favorite of Antonio Scotti, who frequently appeared in it in the role of Chin Fen.

Chinese New Year was but one of the celebrations of Old World groups that at frequent intervals gave the town a festive air. Another was Columbus Day, observed by both the Spanish and Italians, by the first with a banquet and ball, by the second with a blocks-long parade of floats and uniformed marchers which wended its way through the downtown streets and ended at one of the North Beach open spaces, where a succession of speeches, songs, and colorful folk dances, lit by bonfires and flaming torches, lasted far into the night. Yet another was the German October-Fest, when thousands of participants, decked out in gay Bavarian costumes, the men in leather breeches and Alpine hats, the women in brightly colored skirts and velvet jackets, made the long march out to Golden Gate Park and there put on their dances, sang their lusty drinking songs, and consumed prodigious quantities of sausages, kraut, and dark German bread, washed down with copious draughts of beer.

Those mentioned, along with Bastille Day, St. Patrick's, Mexico's *Cinco de Mayo*, Bobby Burns's Birthday, and a long list of others, made the San Francisco of the 1890s a town that, in the words of one bemused visitor, "was always celebrating something or other." As a matter of fact, the residents were never loath to put aside dull workaday cares and seize any excuse—it didn't greatly matter what—to make merry. If no special occasion presented itself, they banded together regardless, during the summer months streaming each Sunday morning aboard the trans-bay ferries, bound for an ascent of Tamalpais over the new serpentine railroad, for picnics in the Marin redwood groves, or for a day of feasting, dancing, and games at one or another of the amusement parks scattered along the bay shore from San Jose north to Vallejo.

The scenes on the ferryboats as these throngs, tired but still hilarious, made their way home were such that few who observed them ever forgot. They marched aboard in a never ending stream and by their very number took possession of the craft, jamming the restaurant and bar below and, led by accordionists or whatever other musicians happened to be present, paraded through the upper deck, singing lustily. Mostly it was good, high-spirited fun, and if—as occasionally happened—rival groups clashed, the casualties were seldom more serious than skinned knuckles, split lips, or blackened eyes.

II.

Then as now, one of the town's favorite recreation spots was "the beach," which daily drew its quota of visitors, in fair weather to stroll on the sands, in foul to gather at the Cliff House and view the antics of the sea lions on nearby Seal Rocks, and rain or shine to take in the wonders of the incomparable Sutro Baths. That structure, covering a full three acres, its walls and roof of glass enclosing six pools of assorted sizes, depths, and temperature was, as the locals were never tired of proclaiming, the largest man-made bathing pavilion in creation.

"A Little of Paris, of Rome, of Pekin"

On fine Sundays the movement toward the beach took on the aspect of a city-wide exodus. First to appear, well in advance of the main body of picnickers and bathers, were the bon vivants, bound for one of the Cliff House's celebrated Sunday breakfasts, stupendous repasts that commonly lasted the better part of the forenoon. These high-livers, traveling either in their own smart carts or four-wheelers, or more prosaically by public hack, made their way through Golden Gate Park—then a waste of sandhills, with only here and there clumps of trees and shrubs giving promise of the luxuriance to come—then up the sandy cliff road to the tavern.

Before these first arrivals had come to the end of their three-hour-long repasts, the advance guard of the hoi polloi had made their appearance. By the mid-1890s these had their choice of two routes from town. One was by electric trolley that rattled and swayed out Clement Street to its end, circled the cliffs above the sea, and deposited its passengers in a big wooden shed just above the baths. While this way afforded them an excellent view of the Golden Gate and even, on clear days, a glimpse of the distant Farallones, most Sunday excursionists—particularly the small fry—chose the alternate route, that via the steam dummy. This, a string of little day coaches, open to the elements and drawn by an ancient locomotive, was boarded at its eastern terminus at the corner of California Street and Presidio Avenue, opposite the end of the California cable line. From there, rocking and bumping over its uneven roadbed, it proceeded out through the sandhills, following Point Lobos Avenue to the beach. There the passengers, grimy with soot and half choked from the smoke of the engine, were deposited before the gates of Adolph Sutro's elegantly landscaped home on the cliff above—all at a cost of five cents, with children under ten carried free.

The dapper, white-whiskered Sutro was then owner of virtually all the area. Having amassed a considerable fortune by promoting a tunnel under Nevada's Comstock Lode, he had shrewdly invested it in numerous tracts of land on the outer perimeter of the town. In the early 1880s he bought the wind-swept plateau above the Cliff House and set about transforming it into a domain worthy of a prince of his native Prussia. His house, a rambling wooden structure, turreted and gabled in the best style of the day, stood at the edge of the cliff, its windows overlooking the coast line for miles to the north and south.

The beautification of the extensive grounds of the Heights —as he termed his estate—became and remained Sutro's major concern. Enclosed on three sides by double rows of cypress trees to break the constant winds, the area was laid out in the manner of an Italian garden, complete with flower beds, fountains, stone balustrades, and garden houses, with groups of statuary placed at intervals beside the glisteningly white walks and driveways. For the better part of a decade a small army of workmen was engaged in these projects, the cost of which the newspapers of the day estimated at a round million dollars.

San Franciscans considered it money well spent. For from the beginning Sutro, no recluse, had thrown the Heights open to the public between the hours of nine and five each day, and the public had responded in force, following the area's transformation from wind-swept hilltop to elegant pleasance with an interest hardly less keen than that of the owner himself. To be sure, there were a few malcontents who grumbled that no man, particularly one who professed to be a friend of the workers—and who, running on that ticket, had recently been elected mayor—had any business surrounding himself with the magnificence of an Oriental potentate.

There were, too, those in the art-conscious town who found

fault with the Heights, not on social or political, but on aesthetic grounds. These pointed out that the scores of statues that ornamented the gardens were none of them locally produced but were merely replicas of woodland nymphs and fauns and dryads copied from European originals; moreover, that the capitalist—who had his frugal side—had had them reproduced not in enduring marble, but in plaster. While this last charge was indeed true, few visitors could see that it made any difference. To be sure, after the winter rains and fogs, the figures took on a somewhat rusty and weathered look, but when spring came around the owner never failed to have them repainted to a dazzling whiteness.

But for all its magnificence, the Heights was not Sutro's only, or indeed his chief, contribution toward making the area a favorite spot for San Franciscans on pleasure bent. For in the mid-1890s he built on the rocky cliffside below his residence the big baths that have ever since borne his name. In addition to its six pools, the great, curving glass roof soared above rows of seats accommodating 7,000 spectators, and on the upper levels broad promenades extended the length of the structure. These last were flanked by cases containing scores of exhibits of an instructive nature: stuffed birds and animals and fishes, historical costumes and documents, curios of various sorts and *objets d'art.*

From the day they were opened the baths became one of the stellar attractions of the town. It was by no means unusual for as many as 25,000 to pass through its turnstiles on fine Sundays, each paying a modest ten cents for the privilege, or, if they wished to bathe, twenty-five cents, which included the rental of a suit.

A few yards down the hill from the baths and perched on the very edge of the precipice, was the Cliff House, the history of which extended back to Civil War days. The original at-

43

traction that had drawn the townspeople to the spot was the group of rocks just offshore, on the surface of which a colony of sea lions could usually be seen cavorting or sunning themselves. For many years the kingpin of the lot was a huge beast known to every San Franciscan as Ben Butler, so named for a widely known politician and orator of the day. When Old Ben presently died, Sutro had his carcass stuffed and placed on display in the museum of the baths up the hill.

When Sutro settled on the Heights, this little resort at the base of the cliff was his nearest neighbor. The original low wooden structure contained a bar, a dining room, and a few chambers for the accommodation of visitors who wished to stay overnight. During the 1860s it could be reached from downtown only via a privately owned route known as the Point Lobos Toll Road. Over this an omnibus, drawn by four horses, made tri-daily trips starting from Portsmouth Plaza, the fare being fifty cents per person each way.

Long the resort's owner and host was a picturesque ex-sea captain named "Pop" Foster. When, sometime in the 1870s, patronage began to fall off, the resourceful Foster installed on the premises a bevy of fair but frail maidens, whereupon business promptly picked up again. Hence, during the next few years, a visit to the Cliff House took on a somewhat different significance in the eyes of the knowing. At that period out-of-town visitors, unaware of the reputation the resort had gained, would sometimes complain to the owner of the bold behavior of these nymphs. Foster's method of handling such situations was to grasp the scandalized guest by the arm, lead him out on the veranda, and dilate eloquently on the beauties of the view.

When Sutro moved into his house above, he purchased the place from Foster, installed a new manager, and issued orders that it thereafter be conducted as a respectable family resort.

That program was faithfully carried out for the better part
of a decade. Then, on Christmas Day of 1894, fire broke out
in the kitchen, made rapid headway, and while crowds gathered from all parts of the city and looked on helplessly, it
burned to the ground. Some two years later, however, Sutro
rebuilt the structure, this time on a far more elaborate scale.

It is this Cliff House, which stood until destroyed by an
even more spectacular fire in 1907, that old-timers like to
recall today. It was a big wooden building hanging over the
very edge of the cliff and a source of wonder to all who be-
held it. Tradition has it that it was patterned after a castle on
the Rhine that many years earlier had aroused the admiration of its then youthful owner. This might well have been
the case, for the structure was a truly extraordinary aggrega-
tion of towers and turrets and gables at which San Franciscans and out-of-towners alike gaped in awe.

Yet another building, the third of the series, was later put
up and continues to occupy the site today. However, when
elderly citizens in reminiscent mood speak nostalgically of the
Cliff House, it is safe to assume that it is Sutro's clapboard
castle, and not the present-day structure, to which they refer.

III.

Throughout the 1890s another favorite recreation spot for
the pleasure-loving populace was Golden Gate Park. When,
in 1869, the city acquired, at a cost of close to a million dollars, that 1,007-acre strip of barren wasteland, there were
those who contended that it had made an extremely bad
bargain. For years thereafter rural editors delighted to poke
fun at that monumental piece of folly on the part of their
city cousins. "Of all the elephants . . . San Franciscans ever

owned," commented one in the mid-1870s, "they now have the largest and heaviest in the shape of 'Golden Gate Park,'" and the writer went on to state that to grow even a blade of grass on that windy waste it would need to be tied to four sturdy posts to prevent its being blown away.

For a time it appeared that these and other dire predictions were likely to be realized. Early attempts to transform its barren sandhills into a sylvan beauty spot were a complete failure, the strong winds that swept in from the ocean burying the trees and shrubs as fast as they could be set out. Only at the eastern end of the four-mile strip was any progress made, and even there it was a constant struggle to keep the driveways and planted areas free of the drifting sand.

It was not until the appointment as superintendent, in 1887, of a dour young Scot named John McLaren that victory was achieved. The real problem was, of course, to find some way of immobilizing the shifting sand that was causing all the trouble. This McLaren solved by importing from his native Scotland a plant bearing the formidable name of *Ammophila arenaria,* which when planted on a sandhill had the quality of pushing its shoots back to the surface as fast as the sand buried them. This process went on until the hill reached a height where the winds could no longer carry the sand to its crest, whereupon the plant spread over its entire surface, anchoring it down permanently.

Because large amounts of fertilizer were necessary to grow trees and flowers and lawns on the areas thus reclaimed, McLaren induced the city's street sweepers to deposit there the wagonloads of manure they daily gathered on the downtown thoroughfares. Accordingly, when in the mid-1890s automobiles began to supplant horse-drawn vehicles, Uncle John—as McLaren had come to be called—viewed that development with dismay. In fact, so strong was his prejudice against the newfangled gas buggies that for several years he succeeded in excluding them from the park, on the pretext that the fumes they emitted were bad for the vegetation adjacent to the driveways.

It was ever Uncle John's aim to make the big area under his care a tree- and flower-studded retreat where city-bound residents could commune with nature unspoiled. Accordingly, he strenuously opposed the placing within its borders of anything that might tend to mar its sylvan peace and quietude. In this, however, he was consistently overruled, and before many years had passed, much of its area was given over to buildings of various sorts, to numerous statues and fountains, plus a bandstand and a race track.

But in his battle against what he considered the spoliation of his park, Uncle John had his minor victories. Thus when, in the early 1890s, the city fathers set aside an acre on its northern boundary and built there a police station, he had a row of young trees planted in front of the structure to hide it from view. On making his rounds a few days later he came on a gang of workmen for the Police Department pulling up his trees and preparing to make a parking area there. He promptly had them replanted. Later that same day he found his trees again uprooted and the workmen pouring cement over the spots where they had stood. McLaren thereupon summoned a crew of gardeners and stood over them while they shoveled the cement out of the holes as fast as the others shoveled it in. In the end the chief of police called off his men and Uncle John triumphantly replanted his trees. This time they remained there permanently and the department's parking lot was laid out in a less conspicuous spot.

When, in the early 1900s, Uncle John reached sixty, and so became eligible for retirement, he flatly refused to leave his beloved park. Ten years later, at seventy—the compulsory retirement age for city employees—he again refused, and this time the Board of Supervisors passed an ordinance not only exempting him from the law but granting him a substantial increase in salary. He continued to hold office and actively direct the affairs of the city park system for more than a quarter century longer, his fifty-six years as superintendent ending only with his death in 1943, at the age of ninety-seven.

Uncle John's long struggle to keep his park free of statues, buildings, hot dog stands, and like blemishes received its severest setback in 1894. This came about because the previous year the Columbian Exposition had been held at Chicago, and the man in charge of the California exhibit there, M. H. de Young, publisher of the *Chronicle,* conceived the idea of holding a second fair at San Francisco, at which many of the attractions on view at Chicago would be shown.

The publisher hurried home and at a mass meeting of citizens some $350,000 was subscribed for the project. This was a remarkable accomplishment, for the city—along with the rest of the country—was then in the midst of a severe depression. Moreover, the other local papers were at best lukewarm toward the project, looking on it as the *Chronicle's* baby. De Young, however, conducted his campaign with shrewdness and vigor, pointing out that by calling the exposition the Midwinter Fair and fixing its opening date as January 1 of the following year, world-wide attention would be called to San Francisco's salubrious winter climate.

When the *Chronicle* proposed holding the fair in Golden Gate Park, Uncle John fought the suggestion tooth and nail, maintaining that to do so would set back for many years his plans for the beautification of the area. However, despite his protests, the site was duly approved by the city authorities, and when ground-breaking ceremonies were held there in the summer of 1893 a sizable crowd—the *Chronicle's* estimate was

80,000, those of other papers much less—was on hand to witness them.

As luck would have it, San Francisco's rainfall that fall was far above average, with successive storms so slowing down construction that many of the buildings were unfinished when January 1 rolled around. Nonetheless, the gates were thrown open on that day and thousands—again their number varies according to which journal one consults—hurried in to see the transformation that had been wrought on the 200-acre site.

They saw more than a hundred buildings grouped about the central Grand Plaza, ranging in size from commodious exhibition pavilions to smaller structures housing the products of states and counties as well as those of several foreign countries. It was, however, the concessions offering visitors entertainment that gained the fair its greatest renown. These included, among others, the Moorish Village, the Japanese Tea Garden, the Vienna Prater, and—easily the prize of the lot—the Turkish Village. For there held forth at frequent intervals throughout the afternoons and evenings a shapely Oriental dancer known as Little Egypt—the first of a series of Little Egypts who were to shock and entrance San Franciscans for the balance of the decade.

The original Little Egypt was brought out from the amusement park of the Chicago fair; however, no less than half a dozen others were presently appearing not only within the fair grounds but in the downtown resorts, each striving to outdo the others by the ribaldry of her act and the scantiness of her costume. In any event, the bevy of dancers helped mightily to draw visitors to the fair from all over the West, and when the gates were closed on July 9, the total attendance figure stood at 2,255,551, more than seven times San Francisco's population at the time.

When the site was cleared and its 200 acres again came under Uncle John's supervision, two of its features were permitted to remain: the Art Museum and the Japanese Tea Garden. The first-named, a lath-and-plaster structure, built in what was described as a "modified Egyptian" style of architecture, long housed a collection of objects ranging from authentic old masters to family heirlooms and relics of gold rush days. The building stood until 1926, when it was declared structurally unsound and torn down. The Japanese Tea Garden, with its picturesque wooden buildings, its grounds planted to the flowers and shrubs of Nippon and dotted with fish pools and quaint bridges, remains to this day one of the most popular of the park's attractions. Few of the thousands who visit it each year realize that it dates from the all but forgotten Midwinter Fair, which closed its gates more than six decades ago.

IV.

Another spot that was much frequented by the fun-loving populace throughout the 1890s was the steep-sided cone of Telegraph Hill, in the lee of which the original town had been laid out. It was so named because in the early days a crude semaphore had stood on its crest by means of which the townspeople were apprised of the passage through the Golden Gate of incoming ships, the position of its arms designating the type of vessel, whether schooner, brig, barkentine, or other variety of windjammer, or steamer.

That the meaning of these signals was known to the entire populace—including small boys—is clear from an incident that was recalled for many years after. During the course of a play at a local theater the hero approached the footlights at one of the high points of the drama and, with arms extended, demanded eloquently, "What does this mean?" The answer brought down the house. For at once the high-pitched voice of a youngster in the gallery was heard shouting excitedly: "Side-wheel steamer!"

By the beginning of the 1890s the early-day semaphore had long since disappeared. In its place stood a baroque wooden structure known as the Castle. This housed a restaurant, bar, and dance hall, and was surmounted by an observation tower from which a sweeping view of the city and bay could be had. To convey visitors to and from this lofty resort a steep, three-block-long cable railroad had been built in the early 1880s. During its first years the Castle, under the management of a former pugilist named Duncan Ross, was a favorite with the town's sports. Charley Mitchell, Paddy Ryan, and other local boxers made it their headquarters while preparing for their fights, and among its visitors was no less a figure than the mighty John L. Sullivan.

Presently, however, the venture came on hard times; patronage dropped off, the cable railroad was abandoned, and for some years the big building stood vacant. It was destined, however, to make a spectacular exit. For in July of 1903 fire broke out and, whipped by brisk summer winds, raced through the building, reducing it to rubble in less than an hour. On its site today stands Coit Tower, the lofty, fluted column that is visible from virtually every part of the city.

Lillie Hitchcock Coit, the donor of this landmark, was one of the bumper crop of picturesque characters whose antics alternately entertained and shocked staid residents all during the second half of the last century. Daughter of an army doctor, Charles M. Hitchcock, eight-year-old Lillie was brought to San Francisco in 1851, spent her childhood and youth in the raw, teeming town, and early showed signs of the unorthodox behavior that was to keep her in the public eye for many years to come.

While living with her parents at the Occidental Hotel at Bush and Sansome streets, it was her habit to make her way each evening to the wooden sidewalk outside, drop a fishing line, its hook baited with a piece of cheese, through a hole in the planks and draw forth a series of rats from the dank depths below. Catching the creatures was an exciting pastime for the young sportswoman, but she could not bring herself to kill them after their capture; however, among the crowd of onlookers who nightly gathered about, there was usually someone who would perform that office.

Throughout that early period fires were frequent in the jerry-built town, no less than five having swept through its central area during the first three years. Because of that ever present danger, the volunteer firemen occupied an honored place in the community and a keen rivalry sprang up among the different companies to be the first to play water on a blaze. At the tolling of the fire bells, it was Lillie's habit to follow the hand-drawn apparatus through the streets and cheer her favorite company, urging its members to be the first on the scene.

The organization to which she gave her allegiance was Knickerbocker Engine Company No. 5, and so loyal was her support that in 1863—when she had just turned twenty—the Knickerbockers elected her to honorary membership and presented her with a handsomely lithographed certificate that ever after remained one of her prized possessions. Membership carried with it the privilege of attending the annual banquets of the company, at which she appeared in full regalia: red flannel shirt and black tie, wide patent leather belt, short black skirt—a full eight inches above the floor!—

and on her shapely head a high-crowned helmet ornamented with the company's big "No. 5" in burnished brass.

As an honorary member she felt it her duty to be on hand at every fire and cheer her company to ever greater efforts. Once the fire bells rang while she was at Grace Church, attending the dress rehearsal of a fashionable wedding at which she was to be bridesmaid. She rushed outside, hailed a passing hack, and hurried to the fire, which proved to be in a building on lower Market Street. No. 5's engine and that of a rival company were already on the scene when she arrived, both playing water on the flames. Lillie, as was her custom, had made her way to the front row of the spectators and was shouting words of encouragement to the Knicker- bockers when a member of the rival company called across to No. 5's men, scornfully terming their fashionably attired supporter a "feather-bedder"—meaning one who liked the glory of being a fire fighter but who refused to share in the discomforts and perils of the calling. By way of answering that canard, the No. 5's pipeman turned his hose full on Lillie, and she—well understanding the significance of his action—gamely stood her ground and, although drenched to the skin, continued to applaud her confreres.

When a city-sponsored fire department was presently set up and the volunteer companies became inactive, Lillie was taken into the Knickerbocker group of veterans, and when- ever she was in the city was an honored guest at its reunion dinners, held on October 17 of each year. Moreover, as long as she lived, she proudly wore a little gold No. 5 emblem given her by "her" company, and until her death in 1929—at the age of eighty-five—she never failed to sign her name thus: "Lillie Hitchcock Coit—5."

It was, however, not alone her championship of the fire fighters that made the younger Lillie one of the town's best-publicized figures. All through the 1860s and early 1870s rarely did a week pass but that some new prank set the tongues of the conventionally minded wagging. One of her characteristic stunts was recalled many years later by a local physician. One day while he and a number of other students at the Lane Medical School were passing the house nearby where Lillie lived, an upstairs window opened and a shapely limb was thrust into view, its owner singing a ballad then popular at a local variety house, its refrain going thus: "Doctor, dear Doctor, come saw off my leg!"

At the time of that exploit the irrepressible Lillie had been married for some years, she having eloped in the fall of 1868 with Howard Coit, who held the responsible position of "caller" at the Mining Exchange. After living together amicably for some years the pair parted; after their separation Coit confided to friends that it had been in effect a bigamous union, his wife being already the spiritual bride of the town's volunteer firemen.

Although she never wavered in her loyalty to the red-shirted smoke-eaters—on her death she left a sizable sum for the erection of a statue to their memory—she had, too, a keen interest in the literary and artistic life of the time. One of her close friends and admirers was F. Bret Harte during the period when that elegant young man was editing the *Overland Monthly*. For a period she seriously considered making a career of belles-lettres, and Harte, who thought highly of her writings, published a number of her stories and poems and insistently called for more. But pushing a pen in solitude held no attractions to one of her gregarious instincts, and in later life she was content to be a patroness of the arts rather than a practitioner.

At her attractive country villa, Larkmead, in the upper Napa Valley, where she spent many summers during the

1880s and 1890s, her weekend guests usually included some of the eminent literary figures then living about the bay. One of the most frequent of these was Joaquin Miller. Like Harte, the picturesque Joaquin professed to think highly of his hostess's talent; once, before a roomful of guests, he remarked fervently: "Thank God, Lillie, you have never tried to write or I would never have had a chance!"

One summer Miller spent several weeks at Larkmead and there wrote a long narrative poem called *The Psalm of Syria*. Often late at night, after the poet had gone to bed, Lillie would occupy herself by making a clean copy of what he had written during the day. This was by no means a simple task, for Miller's handwriting was atrociously bad, so that he himself often had trouble deciphering it. Sometimes Lillie, finding herself stumped, would ask help from other guests who chanced still to be up. On one occasion the entire party struggled for some time over a phrase that seemed to them to read: "God's white tomatoes!" Considered in relation to its context, this completely failed to make sense, and finally the group decided to consult the poet himself. But on being awakened Miller was as puzzled as the others had been. Sitting up in bed, he blinkingly read and reread the passage. At last, however, with a whoop of triumph, he announced the answer: it had not been "God's white tomatoes" he had written but "God's white tomorrows."

In later life Lillie spent much of her time in traveling, returning to San Francisco and Larkmead only at long intervals. She was, however, at her Napa Valley retreat in the fall of 1880 when Robert Louis Stevenson and his bride spent their honeymoon at the abandoned quicksilver mine on nearby Mount St. Helena. Although Stevenson makes no mention of her in *Silverado Squatters*, it is evident that the pair met, for years later Lillie exhibited to friends a long and cordial letter from the author, written from Vailima and recalling their earlier meetings. One regrets that Stevenson failed to include Mrs. Coit in his gallery of Silverado portraits, for few can doubt that his impressions of her would have made entertaining reading.

As time passed, the indomitable Lillie came to occupy a less conspicuous place in the public eye, her earlier escapades forgotten by all but a few old-timers. Soon after the turn of the century, however, she was again projected into the limelight, this time through no choice of her own. In the summer of 1904, while staying at the Palace Hotel, she was one evening entertaining an old friend, a Major McClung, in her suite when a distant relative—whom she had hired to look after her San Francisco properties—entered and, locking the door behind him, drew a revolver and leveled it at her.

Before the intruder could fire, McClung sprang on him, and in the struggle that followed the weapon was discharged, the ball striking the major, who fell to the floor. The crazed man—no reason for his behavior was ever learned—then turned on the lady herself. She, however, far from being cowed, faced his gun unflinchingly, meanwhile calmly reasoning with him, and to such good effect that in the end he pocketed his weapon and hurried downstairs to summon the house physician. Major McClung died the next day and his assailant, having been pronounced insane, was committed to an asylum.

The affair, of course, created a sensation, and to escape the publicity that followed, Mrs. Coit fled to Paris. While there she learned that the demented man had vowed to kill her should he ever regain his freedom; the result was that not until the other's death some twenty years later did she return to San Francisco. She was close to eighty when she finally came back, and so ill that much of the next five years

were spent on a hospital bed, where she died in the summer
of 1929. Today Coit Tower on Telegraph Hill, together with
a statue honoring the volunteer fire fighters of the early town,
in nearby Columbus Square, stands as a memorial to this
most colorful of San Francisco's daughters.

CHAPTER 3

Bohemia's Realm

I.

Long a stronghold of the town's painters, writers, musicians, and other votaries of Art (with or without a capital A) has been the big, four-storied Montgomery Block that for more than a century has stood athwart the lower end of Columbus Avenue opposite the point where that thoroughfare takes off at an angle on its progress through the heart of the Italian quarter.

From the beginning the Block's ground floor has been given over to trade, in its earlier period being occupied by such renowned concerns as the Adams Express Company, the Pacific & Atlantic Railroad, and the offices of two leading journals, the *Alta California* and the *Daily Herald*. At the corner of Washington was the resplendent Bank Exchange, most elegant of the town's bars, boasting a floor of white marble tiles brought round the Horn from Vermont, and dispensing a beverage much fancied by discriminating tipplers of the day, its most potent ingredient being a fiery Peruvian brandy.

Later the original tenants of these street-floor quarters one by one moved out and were replaced by others: the shops of gunsmiths, pawnbrokers, clothing merchants, and, at the corner of Merchant Street, by a series of restaurants, the most famous of which was that of Giuseppe Coppa. The Bank Exchange, however, continued to hold forth for many years, serving its pisco punch to successive generations of San Franciscans until 1920, when the Volstead Act permanently closed its doors.

What gave the Block its unique character, however, was not the commercial establishments on the street level. For rising above were three floors of big, high-ceilinged rooms, the most desirable of which looked out through tall windows on Montgomery and Washington streets, while those on the other side of the broad central corridors opened on an inner court.

When it was put up in 1853, the Block was the largest commercial structure on the entire West Coast and so much in advance of its time that many, convinced that tenants could never be found to fill its more than a hundred rooms, scornfully dubbed it "Halleck's Folly." The reference was to its chief owner, Henry W. Halleck, lawyer and ex-army officer, who, a scant decade later was to become top general of the Union forces during the Civil War. Gloomy predictions that the Block would permanently remain half empty were, however, speedily proved groundless. For immediately on its completion, and for many years thereafter, it was full to capacity. Leading law firms, mining companies, and the agents for eastern financial houses took suites on the Montgomery and Washington street sides, while stockbrokers, real estate operators, and other substantial businessmen occupied quarters elsewhere in the building, well aware of the prestige of a Montgomery Block address.

With the passing of the years, however, and the rise of newer buildings farther down Montgomery and along California and Pine, the more up-and-coming business- and professional men moved into these, and the Block's big, outmoded rooms came to know a quite different sort of tenant: tailors, fortunetellers, Chinese herb doctors, dealers in old clothes, and the like.

Such was the lowly estate to which the building had fallen by the mid-1880s. Toward the end of that decade, however, the beginnings of yet another change in the character of its residents became observable. Drawn by its reasonable rents, its nearness to those low-priced restaurants where the economy-minded Bohemians were wont to dine, and by the fact that the big, outside rooms had excellent light, members of the town's artistic colony began moving in:/painters, sculptors, potters, workers in wood and metal, together with a leavening of poets, musicians, journalists, and free-lance writers. /

One visitor to the Block at the beginning of that period, namely, in the summer of 1888, was a frail Scot whose wizardry with words had in the previous half dozen years won him international renown. Robert Louis Stevenson was in town preparing for what to San Franciscans of the time seemed a highly romantic adventure: a six-month cruise among the more remote islands of the South Seas. The errand that had brought him down to Montgomery Street had to do with the chartering of a vessel in which to make the proposed voyage, he having set his heart on the *Casco*, a trim, 100-foot yacht that belonged to Dr. Henry Merritt, wealthy physician and landowner of Oakland.

Merritt at first was dubious about entrusting his valuable craft to the stranger—authors being notoriously poor business risks—and it was in the hope of overcoming his scruples that

61

he was asked to come over for a personal interview with the applicant. The meeting took place in the second-floor suite of Judge John H. Bolton, eminent member of the local bar and currently serving as president of the Bohemian Club. In the latter capacity Bolton had met Stevenson, had been won over by his high spirits and charm of manner, and had offered his services as mediator. On first arriving at the Block, Dr. Merritt was cool and cautious, and for a time it appeared that nothing would come of the meeting. However, under the influence of the judge's eloquence and Stevenson's good-fellowship, his manner gradually changed, and when the genial Scot was able to produce unassailable proof of his financial soundness, the doctor's last doubts vanished. The deal was consummated and the trio retired to the Bank Exchange downstairs, where a round of toasts was drunk to the success of the expedition.

This, of course, was not Stevenson's first visit to San Francisco or to the Montgomery Block. Almost a decade earlier, unknown, miserably poor, and in wretched health, he had spent some weeks in the town, having traveled by slow steamer and emigrant train from England to join Fanny Osbourne, for whom he had formed a romantic attachment while both were members of an artists' colony in France. At the time of his arrival his inamorata's divorce was still pending, and before they could depart on their honeymoon at Silverado, Stevenson eked out a precarious existence in a rooming house on Bush Street, limiting himself to two frugal meals a day, and, whenever he was strong enough to hold a pen, doggedly producing essays, stories, and articles, which he hopefully forwarded to the editors of English reviews.

His two stays in San Francisco were, hence, an impressive study in contrasts. On his first he was unknown, virtually penniless, and with health so bad that at times his life was despaired of. When he returned he was one of the most widely known writers of his day, far stronger physically, and —with leading journals on both sides of the Atlantic bidding for whatever he wrote—well able to afford the by no means inconsiderable expense of chartering a yacht in which to explore the South Seas.

When Stevenson sailed out the Golden Gate in June of 1889, he was, as it proved, bidding a final adieu to San Francisco. That the friendships he had formed there during his two stays were lasting was, however, demonstrated when, some six years later, word reached town of his death in distant Samoa. At once a group of admirers—artists, writers, architects, and others—began laying plans for a memorial. This—the first of several to be erected to his memory—took the form of a graceful granite pillar, its front bearing an excerpt from his "Christmas Sermon," and surmounted by a bronze galleon under full sail. It was dedicated, with due ceremony, in 1897, and still stands in the center of Portsmouth Plaza, that having been a favorite loitering place for the author during his two stays in the city.

Stevenson's connection with the Montgomery Block was both brief and casual; there were, however, any number of others who through the years were daily to be encountered mounting its marble stairways or striding the length of its big, draughty halls. One of the most familiar of these was Adolph Sutro of Sutro Heights fame, who first took up quarters there in the early 1880s, and who remained long after most of its wealthy tenants had moved elsewhere. Sutro took offices there soon after he came down from Nevada's Comstock Lode following the sale of his widely heralded tunnel. An ardent bibliophile, he had some years earlier begun assembling a collection of scientific books, chiefly those printed during the fifteenth and sixteenth centuries. These volumes he at first stored in his office; presently, however, his collecting ardor increased, and it was not long before his heavy buying on the world's markets made larger quarters imperative. He accordingly leased generous space on the second and third floors, had the floor between torn out, and fitted up the big, high chamber as a library.

There during the next decade he spent a major part of his time, often remaining half the night poring over dealers' catalogues, ordering lavishly, and building toward his goal of a million volumes. For by that time it had become his ambition to assemble the largest—and most valuable—private library on the continent. As his collection grew, even the spacious quarters in the Block became overcrowded, and he laid plans to put up an impressive library building elsewhere in town. Meantime he arranged to have the new shipments that were arriving almost daily stored in a warehouse on nearby Battery Street.

Sutro died in 1898 and the building of the library had to be delayed pending the settlement of his estate. Thus when the fire of 1906 broke out, his valuable collection of incunabula and other early works was directly in the path of the flames. During the first day the Battery Street warehouse and its contents were consumed, and as the wall of destruction advanced toward the Block, the Sutro heirs commandeered wagons and, hastily gathering up several hundreds of the rarest volumes, transported them to the Mechanics' Institute Pavilion at Larkin and Hayes streets. This was on the outer edge of the business district and, so it was thought, well out of the danger zone. However, as events were to demonstrate, that proved a serious mistake of judgment. For on the next day, April 19, the flames, on a mile-wide front, raced through the area to which the books had been taken, whereas the sturdy Block—thanks largely to the firewalls Halleck had incorporated into its design—escaped unscathed. Thus by far the most valuable part of the great Sutro collection was lost.

From the beginning of the 1890s until 1906, the Block had, as stated, sheltered a goodly number of the town's painters, writers, sculptors, and other workers in the arts. After the fire, however, the pressing demand for office space of any sort sent rentals soaring to a point where the former tenants were forced to give way to those better able to pay: insurance firms, railroad and steamship companies, and the like. Thus for a year or two the venerable Block once more sheltered some of the town's most renowned business concerns. Eventually, though, with the rehabilitation of some of the fire-gutted downtown structures and the erection of new ones, the intruders moved out. Thereupon, its big, barnlike rooms were once more taken over by the sons and daughters of Bohemia, who have remained there ever since.

II.

Although the Sutro library, due to its owner's death and the losses it sustained in 1906, was never made available to scholars of the period, the town was by no means lacking in such facilities, either during the 1890s or earlier. Indeed, almost from the beginning residents had prided themselves on the fact that, for all its distance from the old-established centers of learning, theirs was no crude, unlettered frontier camp. In proof of that contention they rarely failed to point out that as early as 1851 more daily newspapers were being published locally than in London; that the city's well-stocked bookstores had no lack of patrons, and its two literary journals, the *Pioneer* and the *Golden Era*, were both ably edited and widely read.

Thus, when, in the mid-1870s, a British visitor termed it a "city of newspaper readers," San Franciscans were quick to take offense at what they considered a reflection on the breadth of their reading interests, and the journals of the day blossomed out with indignant denials of the canard. One letter writer in the *Alta* maintained that the townspeople owned—and read—more books per capita than those of any other community of its size in the country, and challenged the visitor to name a town of comparative population in England that had as many large and well-selected libraries, both public and private.

Among the collections cited by this writer was that of the Mercantile Library, an organization that since its founding in 1852 had had a singularly eventful history. During the first decade and a half of its existence it occupied a number of sites in the downtown area; then, having raised some $20,000 by the sale of life memberships, it bought a lot on Bush Street between Montgomery and Kearny and erected on it a handsome five-story building, into which it moved in 1868.

In so doing, the library incurred an indebtedness of close to a quarter of a million dollars, and it was in the hope of paying this off that the directors came up with a scheme which was to cause heated discussion for years afterward. This was to be no less than a series of lotteries, tickets to which would be sold throughout the city and the drawings held in the big, barnlike pavilion of the Mechanics' Institute in Union Square. Lotteries being illegal in California, the directors had a bill introduced in the state legislature at Sacramento authorizing "the public entertainments, at which personal property, real estate or other valuables might be disposed of, by chance, raffle, or other scheme of like character." Despite strong opposition on the part of church groups and others, the bill was passed toward the close of 1870 and promptly received the governor's signature.

The drawings were held the following summer, and gala occasions they proved to be. On each of the three nights an elaborate program of entertainment was provided for the thousands who packed the auditorium. Scant attention was paid to the performers, however, for the audiences were looking forward to the drawings that were to follow. During the hour-long raffles a wide variety of prizes were passed out. These ranged from hats, gloves, and other articles of wearing apparel, on through jewelry, musical instruments, and sets of books, to stylish phaetons and teams of thoroughbred horses, winding up each night with the award of a handsome, bay-windowed residence, completely furnished, in one of the newer districts to the west of Van Ness Avenue.

From a financial standpoint the venture was a resounding success, yielding a profit of some $310,000. But the means employed—"an out-and-out gaming device," charged its critics—alienated many former friends of the organization, and thereafter it never occupied quite the same place in the regard of a large and influential segment of the population. A few years later it sold its Bush Street property and moved to a building on the corner of Golden Gate and Van Ness avenues. This, however, was a less convenient location than the old one and patronage continued to fall off. Nonetheless, it remained open for close to a decade longer, then its books— numbering some 100,000 volumes—plus its extensive files of early San Francisco newspapers, were combined with another pioneer organization, the Mechanics' Institute.

The Institute, which likewise dated from the 1850s, had long played a prominent part in the cultural and business life of the town. Not only did it maintain a well-stocked library, but for many years it sponsored a series of annual fairs at which were exhibited both the products of local industries and the works of the town's artists. To house these it built a number of large pavilions that were used, too, for concerts, political rallies, and other public assemblages. Early in its existence the Institute established its library and reading room on Post Street between Market and Kearny, a site on which, after the 1906 fire, it put up the substantial, nine-story building it occupies today.

San Francisco's libraries, however, were by no means its only citadels of learning. For notwithstanding its hedonistic philosophy, the tendency on the part of the average citizen to take his pleasures where he found them, however unsubstantial or transitory they might be, the town was never without its groups of earnest souls who preferred to spend their leisure hours pursuing more serious—and presumably more rewarding—ends.

Thus throughout the decade of the 1890s it had its full share of organizations devoted to scholarly purposes, literary, scientific, and historical. Among the most active of these were the Society of California Pioneers and the California Historical Society, the first-named dating from 1850 and, thanks to the generosity of the early-day capitalist, James Lick, occupying spacious quarters on Pioneer Place, an alley off Fourth Street, a few yards from Market.

Lick was also the prime benefactor of the California Academy of Sciences, which, like the Pioneer Society, dated from the early 1850s. In 1891 the Academy moved into its own building on Market Street above Fourth, a gift of the capitalist, who had recently died. There for the next fifteen years it maintained both a museum and an extensive collection of the flora and fauna of the lands bordering on the Pacific. Among other scientific bodies flourishing during that period were the Geographical Society of the Pacific, of which the many-sided George Davidson was long the guiding spirit, and the Astronomical Association.

Of the many organizations, loosely termed literary societies, that were intermittently active throughout the 1890s, one of the most interesting, and long-lived, was that which termed itself the Chit-Chat Club. Founded in 1874, with membership limited to twenty-four, it met monthly for dinner, followed by the reading of a paper on some recondite subject prepared by one of the members. This program the club has, with admirable consistency, carried out to the present day, one of its proudest boasts being that in all the eighty-odd years of its existence it has never missed a meeting.

To keep that record intact has on occasion required a bit of doing, notably at the time of the earthquake and fire of April 18, 1906. However, the Chit-Chatters proved equal even to that emergency. With the whole central part of the city wiped out and all in confusion, its secretary nonetheless proceeded with plans for the May meeting. Somehow he managed to reach a majority of the members and on the appointed evening they assembled in a bedroom of a house beyond the burned area, its occupant having accommodatingly removed his bed for the occasion. There they sat down to an ample dinner—oysters on the half shell, crab à la poulette, an entree, a Roman punch, dessert, and coffee—prepared in a makeshift kitchen set up on the sidewalk outside, then listened while the speaker of the evening read his paper. The subject of his discourse is, unfortunately, no longer of record, but the speaker, one Hengstler, was a man of wide erudition and one is safe in assuming that it was fully up to the high literary and scholarly standards of the group.

This, however, was not the only occasion on which the serious-minded scholars of the town refused to permit extraneous events to distract them from the orderly pursuit of knowledge. A full half century earlier, in 1856, Dr. Andrew Randall, president of the newly organized California Academy of Sciences, was shot down by one Joseph Hetherington, member of a band of thugs then terrorizing the town. The murderer was brought before the Second Vigilance Committee and sentenced to death, and on the evening of the day he was hanged from a gallows set up in Portsmouth Plaza, surviving members of the Academy met at their Clay Street quarters nearby and gravely discussed the merits of two recent publications in their field: Michaux and Nuttall's *North American Sylva*, and a pamphlet dealing with the coniferous trees of California.

Interest in scholarly matters remained high throughout the 1890s, and this despite the fact that when the decade began facilities for higher education in the area were limited. A year was to pass before the new stone buildings on Senator Stanford's former wheat field down the peninsula were to open their doors, and across the bay the long-established University of California still had but seventeen full professors, five associates, six assistants, and nine instructors. But what the Berkeley institution's faculty lacked in numbers was made up for by the caliber of its members. For among them were Joseph Le Conte, geologist of national renown, George Davidson, eminent geographer, Eugene W. Hilgard, agricultural chemist, Andy Lawson, William Carey Jones, and half a dozen others.

Long one of the shining lights of the Berkeley campus was Charles Mills Gayley, head of the English Department and author, among other scholarly works, of *Classic Myths in English Literature*. That thick volume, which for a generation after was known to numberless high school students across the country, elevated its author to such affluence that at one time he was offered the presidency of the Commercial Bank of Berkeley.

However, Gayley preferred to keep his academic post, and he remained head of the department until his retirement, at the age of sixty-five, in the early 1920s. During his long teaching career he had a hand in the development of a numerous group of authors, among them Frank Norris, Jack London, James Hopper, Richard Walton Tully, Eleanor Gates, and many others.

Gayley fully conformed to the popular idea of how a college professor should behave, and many were the stories of his absent-mindedness. One relates that on his return to his Berkeley home after several months' absence in the East, his wife came back from a shopping tour just as he was climbing the stairs to his study. "Hello, dear," he greeted her casually, continuing his ascent. "Have a pleasant walk?"

III.

The fact that the town had its quota of libraries, scientific societies, and organizations of like nature did not, of course, mean that its residents of scholarly or artistic interests took themselves and their work so seriously that they failed to relax and have a good time. On the contrary, they, along with other citizens of the fun-loving city, were ever ready to put aside dull business or professional cares and enjoy themselves to the full. Thus there were nightly gatherings in one or another of the score or more restaurants along Montgomery, Washington, and Jackson streets and elsewhere in the quarter, in its even more numerous bars, and in the studios of its working artists.

Moreover, in addition to such informal gathering places,

there has existed since the early 1870s an organization that provided a common meeting place for all workers in the arts; namely, the Bohemian Club. In the beginning its members met at different restaurants of the area; later they shared quarters for a year or two with a carefree group who—appropriately, it would seem—called themselves the Jolly Corks. Finally, in 1877, the Bohemians moved into rooms of their own on Pine Street, above the California Market.

By the time the 1890s rolled around, the club had made yet another move, this time into quarters at 130 Post Street, between Kearny and Dupont. Meanwhile it had grown in size and prestige, numbering among its members as imposing an array of artists, writers, musicians, and actors—both amateurs and professionals—as any city in the country could boast.

Among painter members were such locally well-known figures as Jules Travernier, landscapist, Amede Joullin, specialist in portraits, William Keith (whose studio was around the corner at 115 Kearny), Tom Hill, creator of huge canvases of Yosemite and other natural wonders of the West, Thad Walch, Charles Rollo Peters, Will Sparks, Arthur Mathews, Joe Strong (son-in-law of Mrs. Robert Louis Stevenson), Julian Rix, and a host of others.

The list of writer members was even longer, ranging from such old-timers as Dan O'Connell and George Bromley, both of whom had been ornaments of the club since its founding, on through Edward Robson Taylor, physician, lawyer, and poet, who later became mayor of the town, Joaquin Miller, Charles Warren Stoddard, Clay Greene, Ambrose Bierce, Arthur McEwen, Prentice Mulford, down to a numerous band of young writers just coming to public notice.

This last-named group was a remarkable one to have been produced in the by no means large town during the course of a single decade. It included Frank Norris and, presently, Jack London, both on the threshold of notable careers, Will and Wallace Irwin, fresh out of Senator Stanford's new university at Palo Alto, Gelett Burgess, draughtsman turned artist and writer, James Hopper, ex-football star at Berkeley, Paul Shoup, short-story writer who wound up as president of the Southern Pacific Railroad, Porter Garnett, noted alike for his elegant prose and for the fact that he was the first local dandy to sport a Van Dyke, and George Sterling and Edwin Markham, a pair of young Oaklanders ambitious to become poets.

During the heyday of the club's renown as a literary and artistic center, workers in related fields were almost as numerous. Among scholars, drawn mainly from the two universities of the area, were such figures as H. Morse Stephens, historian, Joseph Le Conte, geologist, John Muir, naturalist, the poet Edward Rowland Sill, and historians John S. and Theodore Hittell. Sculptor members included Robert I. Aitken, Arthur Putnam, whose depictions of California animals won him national renown, and Douglas Tilden, highly talented deaf-mute.

At its Post Street quarters there congregated throughout that period not only local workers in the arts and allied fields but a goodly number of distinguished guests who chanced to be passing through town. Thus a succession of noted actors, lecturers, novelists, poets, and humorists were entertained there, and left to spread abroad the fame of the town's unique literary and artistic club. In their entertainment of such guests members spared no pains to make the events memorable ones. On one occasion, however, their carefully laid plans backfired. When Oscar Wilde arrived in 1882, a group of members, accomplished trenchermen all, invited him to the club for the express purpose of "drinking him under the table." They had, as events proved, sadly misjudged their man. Throughout the long evening the imperturbable aesthete matched his hosts drink for drink. The latter, one by one, dropped out, and at its end Wilde alone remained upright at the table calmly enjoying a nightcap before making his way back to his hotel to bed.

Early in its existence the club acquired a picturesque grove of redwoods on the Russian River, some sixty miles north of San Francisco. There each summer members and their guests spent a convivial week camping out under the immense trees. The high point of these summer encampments was the production of the annual grove play, every phase of which, from the writing of words and music, the personnel of cast and orchestra, and the design and lighting of the scenery, was done by members.

Thus during the week at the grove men who for the balance of the year earned their living as doctors, lawyers, merchants, artists, and the like, became playwrights, actors, musicians, directors, property men, and supers, finding an outlet for musical, dramatic, and other talents usually unsuspected by their associates in the business or professional world. Moreover, their productions, by and large, had a competence and finish rarely attained by amateurs. Thus the club played a by no means unimportant role in fostering the artistic and literary qualities that since its beginnings have been a part of the city's heritage.

There were, of course, numerous other places where the town's artists—along with the rest of the pleasure-loving populace—were accustomed to foregather. One of these was its hotels, of which the San Francisco of the 1890s had a far greater number than other cities of its size throughout the country. This, like certain other features of its community life, was a direct result of the unusual circumstances

74

of its founding. For during its early years—which after all were then but a scant four decades in the past—private residences were few, the great majority of the predominantly male population living in hotels or rooming houses and eating their meals at restaurants. That habits thus formed were slow to die out is indicated by the fact, often commented on by new arrivals, that block after block in the downtown area was occupied by hostelries of all sizes and conditions, and that all seemed full to capacity.

Strangers were impressed, too, by the imposing array of hotel buses that, day or night, greeted them on their arrival at the Ferry Building. "All was exciting and a bit terrifying," wrote one newcomer, eighteen-year-old Helen MacKnight, who had journeyed down from a little Sierra mining town to enroll in a local medical school—an almost unheard-of proceeding for a woman during the early 1890s. Incoming travelers, having made their way off the boat and through the ramshackle old ferry shed—the handsome new structure was not built until several years later—emerged into what one English globe-trotter termed "bedlam incarnate."

Stretching for many yards to the left and right was a confused jumble of clanging streetcars, both horse-drawn and cable, shouting newsboys, hack drivers, and agents for a dozen different products and services, while backed up to the curb were long rows of buses, each with a runner bent on steering guests to his own vehicle and away from those of his competitors. Cries of "Russ House," "Occidental," "Palace," "Lick House," "Cosmopolitan," "Grand," and half a dozen others filled the air, each man trying to outshout his rivals while he pounced on likely-looking prospects and, seizing their hand baggage, shouldered his way through the crowd, his victims having perforce to follow, if only to retrieve their belongings.

The town's leading caravansary and, despite the fact that it had been built a quarter century earlier, still numbered among the most luxurious in the country, was, of course, the Palace. Occupying an entire block and rising to a height of seven stories, its bay-windowed façade was visible for miles, a civic landmark in which every San Franciscan took pride. By the opening of the 1890s, however, what had been its most striking feature—the lofty inner court into which arriving guests were driven—had been transformed into a palm-studded lounge, the clatter of horses' hoofs on the driveway having set up echoes that had disturbed the rest of those whose rooms opened onto the balconies above.

While the Palace was, and remained until its destruction in 1906, the premier hostelry of the town—and indeed of the entire West Coast—there were a number of other first-class houses, each catering to its own clientele. Across New Montgomery Street from the Palace, and joined to it by a bridge at the second-floor level, stood the older Grand, much favored by theatrical folks. A block distant, at the southwest corner of Montgomery and Sutter, was the Lick House, put up in the early 1880s by ex-cabinetmaker James Lick, who had personally fashioned the intricate woodwork of its dining room; this was long a favorite stopping place for visiting mining men.

Diagonally across from the Lick House was the Occidental, its four stories extending the full block from Sutter to Bush; the Occidental catered to the army and navy set. Further down Montgomery stood the Russ House, on land that its owner, Christian Russ, had bought in 1847 for $37.50, and which had long been frequented by ranchers and cattlemen. Then, on the outer fringe of the business district were numerous "family" hotels catering to permanent guests. One of the most pretentious of these was the Pleasanton at Sutter and Jones streets, tenanted mainly by prosperous citizens who preferred its housekeeping suites to maintaining houses of their own in the residential districts farther out.

One spectacular happening as the decade of the 1890s drew toward its close was the burning in the early-morning hours of November 22, 1898, of another of the town's leading hotels. This was the Baldwin, a rambling, six-story structure that occupied the Market-Powell-Ellis street gore. Built in the mid-1870s—the same period that saw the rise of its bigger but no more ornate rival, the Palace—the Baldwin had long catered to a quite different clientele, it being a favorite stopping place for theatrical people and members of the sporting fraternity.

One reason why this was so is fairly obvious, for its owner was E. J. "Lucky" Baldwin, who, having made a fortune speculating in shares of the Comstock mines, proceeded to devote his abundant energies to managing a string of race horses and, between times, to entertaining the more comely— and compliant—lady members of visiting theatrical troupes.

For a feature of the Baldwin was that its spacious bay-windowed walls enclosed a theater, one, moreover, that got the cream of the touring road shows. Known at first as Baldwin's Academy of Music, it over the years saw such illustrious mimes as John McCullough, Clara Morris, Rose Coghlan, Mary Anderson, Henry Irving, Ellen Terry, Lillian Russell, James K. Hackett, Nat Goodwin, Eddie Foy, John Drew, Maurice Barrymore, William Gillette, Otis Skinner, and a long list of others—a veritable roll call of the great names of the period.

Its manager during much of that time was Tom Maguire, picturesque ex-cabby, whose Opera House on Washington Street had long been a favorite of the theater-going populace. When the building of newer houses farther uptown at length put him out of business at that location, Maguire took charge of the Baldwin and operated it with conspicuous success for

77

some years, one of his specialties being the organization and training of stock companies that played there during periods between traveling shows.

On Maguire's departure for the East in the late 1870s, he was succeeded by one Kelly, like his predecessor a former cab driver and more recently the owner of a livery stable. During Kelly's regime he hired as prompter, part-time actor, and general utility man a stage-struck youth named David Belasco. A second youth who was taken on by Kelly was eighteen-year-old Julius Kahn, who in the spring of 1879 scored a notable success in the role of Shylock. A few years later Kahn abandoned the stage in favor of politics. After holding a variety of minor offices he, in 1898, was elected to Congress and continued to serve his native city in that capacity until his death more than a quarter century later.

Baldwin's combination hotel and theater was long considered a fire hazard, particularly the theater, which could be reached only by a long, narrow foyer opening on Market Street. But the fire laws of the day were lamentably lax, and Baldwin, though a prodigal spender in other directions—his cash settlements on parting from various ladies of the theater were said to have set new standards of liberality—could not bring himself to provide adequate exits from his playhouse.

Nonetheless, the hotel remained Baldwin's pride and joy throughout the twenty-odd years of its existence, and he kept a sharp eye on every phase of its operation. The handsomely appointed bar was his particular favorite and he was ever at pains to see that its patrons behaved with decorum. There were numerous occasions when the brawny owner personally assumed the role of bouncer, ejecting customers who had grown overnoisy or otherwise obstreperous.

Fortunately the fire that eventually destroyed the big structure broke out in the early-morning hours, when the theater, bar, and other public rooms were deserted. Although there were countless narrow escapes among the newly aroused guests, all save one were finally led to safety.

IV.

Long one of the town's show places was the Diamond Palace in the old Russ House, a four-story wooden hotel that covered the entire block on Montgomery Street between Bush and Pine. This, as its name implied, was a jewelry store; indeed, it was *the* jewelry store of the town, the one at which the wives, daughters, and—not infrequently—the mistresses of affluent citizens indulged their taste for rings, brooches, lockets, and similar trinkets and, on occasion, such costly merchandise as pearl necklaces, gem-studded coronets, and diamond tiaras.

Although the Diamond Palace occupied a single narrow room, its canny owner, known to the entire town as "Colonel" Andrews, had created an illusion of spaciousness by lining its walls from floor to ceiling with an unbroken expanse of mirrors, so that one, on entering, saw its row of chaste showcases repeated on both sides until they were seemingly lost in the distance.

Through the final three decades of the century its reputation stood so high that when the wearer of some admired bauble was able to state that "Colonel" Andrews had himself helped pick it out, there could be no greater guarantee of its quality and good taste. But the esteem in which San Franciscans held the shop sprang not alone from the high caliber of its merchandise and the glittering setting in which it was displayed, but equally from the appearance and bearing of the proprietor himself. For the "Colonel"—no one knew where

79

he had picked up the title, but all agreed that it fitted him to perfection—was by no means the least ornamental feature of the place. Erect and tall, his hair and Van Dyke trimmed to perfection, he greeted customers decked out in black cutaway coat and striped trousers, his snow-white linen set off by an impeccable black ascot tie, the one touch of color being the white carnation he invariably wore in his buttonhole.

The elegant owner made no secret of the fact that his establishment catered exclusively to the carriage trade, and the ladies who belonged to that exalted class would go to no other. For, as one Nob Hill matron put it, "Trading at the Diamond Palace, even though one visited it only to have a necklace restrung or the clasp of a locket repaired, bore no resemblance to an ordinary business transaction, for the polite and charming 'Colonel' Andrews lifted each visit to the level of a social call."

Few of the local artists and writers were, for obvious reasons, patrons of the Diamond Palace. They had, however, their favorite gathering places, among which were the town's bookshops. During most of the 1890s the most highly regarded of these was that of William Doxey, centrally located on the Market Street side of the Palace Hotel. Its owner, a genial little Englishman who had arrived some twenty years earlier, was highly popular with residents of Nob Hill and the Western Addition, with the result that, in words of a competitor, "he long enjoyed the best trade, from the best families."

However, the real importance of Doxey's shop lay not in providing currently popular novels and calfbound sets of Dickens, Thackeray, and Bulwer-Lytton to the grande dames of the town, but in quite another direction. For Doxey had kept in close touch with literary trends abroad, not only in his native London but in Paris, Berlin, and elsewhere, and his was the only shop where one could be sure of finding the latest works of the advanced writers of the day, together with such precedent-breaking periodicals as the *Yellow Book* and its imitators.

This, of course, drew to his establishment those local scribblers who were themselves striking out on new paths, among them the group that termed themselves "les Jeunes." The result was that Doxey became a sponsor of the curious little magazine, the *Lark*, which les Jeunes presently launched, and remained its publisher during the two years of its existence.

Because of the stir that precedent-shattering journal made in literary and artistic circles, both locally and further afield, during its brief career, it seems desirable here to sketch its history in some detail. For it has been asserted—with some degree of truth—that it was the means by which the attention of the balance of the country was first directed toward what had been from the beginning the town's position as the intellectual and cultural center of the entire West Coast. To be sure, it had long been recognized that two bright ornaments of American letters, Mark Twain and Bret Harte, had lived in the city at the offset of their careers, Twain but briefly and Harte for a longer period; moreover, that the early numbers of the *Overland Monthly*, under Harte's editorship, had been admired by discriminating readers all over the land. However, that facet of the city's life did not come to be widely recognized elsewhere until the appearance, in the mid-1890s, of this unorthodox, high-spirited little magazine.

The *Lark's* founder and guiding spirit throughout its twenty-four numbers was a young Bostonian named Gelett Burgess, a graduate of the Massachusetts Institute of Technology who had come West in the late 1880s and found a berth as a draughtsman for the Southern Pacific Railroad. After three years at that company's big brick headquarters at Fourth and Townsend streets, Burgess had moved across the bay to Berkeley, where he became an instructor of topographical drawing at the University of California.

However, his stay there was brief, and the incident that ended his teaching career is still recalled by old-time residents. One night Burgess and several cronies, their artistic sensibilities affronted by the statue of a local philanthropist that stood at the juncture of California and Market streets, procured a rope and, tugging mightily, managed to topple it from its base. The likeness was that of Dr. Henry Cogswell, who had embellished the city with numerous other cast-iron monuments, all having fountains offering passers-by the solace of pure Spring Valley water, the donor being an ardent prohibitionist.

That prank having terminated his academic career, Burgess moved to San Francisco, took rooms in a house high on Russian Hill, and found employment designing *fin de siècle* furniture for a local manufacturer. It was shortly thereafter that he, along with three young friends, Willis Polk, Bruce Porter, and Porter Garnett, sent the *Lark* on its initial flight.

"With the hundred dollars that was our entire capital," Burgess later recalled, "we started the venture. The make-up should be original from paper to typography, and we ransacked Chinatown . . . for materials. Here we found cheap but interesting paper of bamboo fibre which was imported in bales, each sheet double folded and stencilled upon the edges with red and green characters. All this had to be unfolded, dampened and pressed, with the result that the sheets were mildewed with strange yellow spots, and around the edges were smears of red and green dye. We set the pages without 'justifying' the lines of type, letting them run out where they would, like typewritten matter, and, as the paper was thin, we printed upon only one side, in the Japanese manner . . ."

Having made sure that the *Lark's* appearance would set it

apart from the conventional magazines of the day, they applied themselves to achieving a like originality in its contents. How well they succeeded is a matter of record. From its first number the little journal broke new ground, the editors making no concessions to orthodox standards, and filling its pages with whatever fancies their imaginations could dream up, however absurd they might seem to literal-minded readers. The result was that while the public at large, after a single glance at its recondite text and odd make-up, decided that the *Lark* was not for them, there were those who found its high-spirited nonsense and shrewd comment on the passing scene exactly to their taste and welcomed it with delight.

In the beginning the number of such readers was small indeed, in the home town or elsewhere. Its first several issues were, so far as its sponsors could observe, completely ignored. The local magazine distributors refused to handle it; the newspapers maintained an unbroken silence, and—as Burgess later wrote—even at the Bohemian Club, "from which by its name and the literary character of its foundation, one might expect some encouragement . . . it was consigned as regularly as it appeared in a table drawer in a faraway corner of the Library."

Nonetheless, the paper at length began to find its intended audience—the "one in ten" its founders hoped would recognize, and perhaps even applaud, what they were trying to do. As time went on, other local writers and artists—and some further afield—joined in the enterprise. One of the earliest of these was the etcher, Ernest Peixotto, who returned from Paris later in 1895 and for some time provided striking drawings for each issue. When Peixotto moved on to New York, his place was taken by Florence Lundborg, who contributed, too, a series of interest-attracting advertising posters. Others who at one time or another contributed to its columns were, besides Burgess, Porter, and Garnett, Willis Polk, Maynard Dixon, Carolyn Wells, Yone Noguchi, and Juliet Wilbor Tompkins.

Burgess himself, however, was mainly responsible for the *succès d'estime* the little journal presently came to enjoy. To each number he supplied both "art work" and reading matter, the latter often appearing under a nom de plume. One of his earliest contributions was a four-line nonsense verse that was soon being quoted throughout the land. So popular did this become, and so often was it recited in its author's presence, that two years later in the *Lark's* final number, he published this sequel:

> Ah, yes, I wrote the "Purple Cow"—
> I'm sorry, now, I wrote it;
> But I can tell you Anyhow
> I'll kill you if you Quote it!

In their way Burgess's illustrations were as amusing as his verses, featuring odd-looking creatures with oversized heads and formless bodies which he called "Goops." In the accompanying texts the Goops were divided into two classes: the sulphites (original thinkers), and the bromides, who parroted the commonplace sayings of others. Both these became popular slang terms in their day, and one—bromides—presently found its way into the dictionaries, it being used to designate a boring person or trite statement. In its brief career the *Lark* contributed yet another word to the language—"blurb," which ever since has been widely used in publishing circles to describe the advertising matter appearing on book jackets.

By the end of its first year the little monthly had attained a circulation of 3,000 copies, at which figure it stood as long as it continued to be published. In the beginning its price was five cents a copy or one dollar a year—Burgess, as he later confessed, had never been good at mathematics. At the end of the first twelve numbers, however, the single-copy price was raised to ten cents, with the yearly subscription remaining the same.

Advertising was for the most part shunned, the only exceptions being occasional notices of books for sale at the shop of the publisher and, in No. 5, a full page taken by Harrold, Belcker & Allen, the firm for which the editor was working as a designer. This stated concisely: "Old furniture made new. New furniture made old. Middle-aged furniture preserved. Black walnut furniture destroyed." Burgess was suspected of having written that copy; he almost certainly wrote a number of other pseudo ads that appeared from time to time, clever take-offs on the style and methods of the copy writers of the day. One was a grave announcement of a forthcoming book by architect Willis Polk, a massive tome entitled *Architecture Moderne*, the edition of which was to be limited to three copies, each handsomely bound in "half-chicken leather."

The Purple Cow was followed by a number of other Burgess verses, some long, as in the case of *The Chewing-Gum Man*—which occupied several pages in the third number—others much briefer, and all illustrated by drawings of the editor's queer-looking Goops. Typical of these was a limerick that appeared beneath a drawing showing a Goop leaping across a room suspended in mid-air:

> I wish that my room had a floor!
> I don't so much care for a door,
>   But this crawling around
>   Without touching the Ground
> Is getting to be quite a Bore!

As the *Lark* neared the end of its second year it seemed well on its way to a long and moderately prosperous existence, with a small but loyal band of readers scattered across the country, with the town's newspapers regularly saluting each issue as it appeared, and with some of the august literary journals of the East Coast praising its sprightliness and originality. It was precisely at that point that Burgess and his confreres decided to close up shop. Years later he explained their reasons for that step. "Our mood," wrote he, "was too spontaneous, or rather too enthusiastic, to last, for we had dwelt over-long with gayety; there was the world's sober work to do. And, jealous of the *Lark's* prestige, which had suffered from no carelessness in our devotion, after two years of the frolic, we brought the essay to a close before it could be said that the fire of our initial enthusiasm had grown cold."

So with a final number, the *Epi-Lark*, which appeared in May of 1897, les Jeunes disbanded and went their separate ways. Burgess headed for New York, then for London and, after a long career as novelist, humorist, and creator of comic drawings, he returned to California and there spent his final years, dying at Carmel as recently as 1951. Bruce Porter became a widely known painter of murals and designer of stained-glass windows; many examples of his work in both mediums are to be seen today in San Francisco churches and other buildings. Willis Polk went on to design, in California and elsewhere, buildings of such originality and distinction as to place him near the top of his profession, and artist Maynard Dixon's canvases won him a place among the foremost interpreters of the Old West. The three women members of the group, Florence Lundborg, Carolyn Wells, and Juliet Wilbor Tompkins, each achieved a degree of fame, the first as a painter, the second as a writer of light verse, and the third as a widely read author of fiction.

The fact that during its brief existence the *Lark* had under its wing so talented a group is one reason why San Franciscans of the present day still recall it with nostalgia. But not the only reason, for the wit, irony, and lighthearted nonsense that so delighted those of the mid-1890s make no less entertaining reading today.

CHAPTER 4

Gourmet's Delight

I.

During the gold rush and for a full decade thereafter, San Franciscans, by and large, knew little and cared less about the manner in which their food was prepared and served. There is ample evidence that in his eating, as in his drinking, the average resident was content with whatever was put before him, provided only that it was sufficient in quantity and of a nature that permitted it to be quickly consumed. The times were far too hectic to permit dawdling over the dining table.

Throughout that period visitors from the genteel centers of the East Coast or Europe were impressed, but by no means entranced, by the viands placed before them, not alone in the leading hotels, restaurants, and clubs, but in the homes of prosperous citizens. It was, as some of these critics made clear, not because of any lack of variety that the meals fell short, for the markets abounded in such game as wild ducks, turkey, and geese, in quails and doves and snipe, trout from the mountain streams, salmon and sole and sand dabs from the waters of the bay, plus deer meat, grizzly steaks, and abundant beef and pork and mutton. The trouble was that when these potential delicacies, having passed through the hands of the unimaginative hirelings in the kitchen, reached the table, their subtle flavors had all too often been fried or boiled or roasted out of them.

The foundations of the town's later fame as an epicure's Elysium were laid when, in the 1870s and early 1880s, certain rich men with interests in western mines, railroads, lumber, and other enterprises came out to inspect their holdings; they frequently traveled in private cars and brought their own chefs. The latter, charmed at the abundance of game, fishes, and other products available in the local markets—and appalled at the manner in which they were prepared and served —saw an opportunity not only to confer a badly needed boon on the townspeople, but to launch themselves in lucrative businesses. In more than one instance the result was that the private cars of the tycoons rolled back across the continent with vastly inferior cooks presiding over their kitchens, the former occupants having remained behind, deep in preparations to open authentic French restaurants.

Tradition has it that this was the origin of three resorts that were widely patronized all through the 1890s, namely, the Maison Riche, the Maison Dorée, and the Poodle Dog. The last-named, which occupied an ancient building at the corner of Pine and Dupont, was originally called the Poulet d'Or and had a handsomely gilded fowl above its doorway. The pronunciation of the name, however, proved difficult to its predominantly non-Gallic patrons, and it was accordingly changed to Poodle Dog. Three blocks farther down Dupont toward Market was the Maison Riche, with entrances both on Dupont and Geary, while the third, the Maison Dorée, was on Kearny between Sutter and Bush.

It was mainly at these three establishments that San Franciscans came to know and appreciate the piquant sauces, subtle flavorings, and related legerdemain by which the French chefs transformed what had been dull, uninspired cookery into something quite different. Those citizens who from the first had prided themselves on the fact that they demanded, and got, the best in all things were not slow to avail themselves of these pleasurable new experiences. They crowded their dining rooms from the day of their opening, tasting the delights of *caviar sur canane, paupiettes de bass, raye à la Normande, poulet de grain aux cresson,* and a dozen other creations, meantime developing a taste for the more renowned French dinner wines and a knowledge of their best vintage years.

These French cafés introduced into the lives of the local bon vivants not only a taste for meals expertly prepared and served, but another and quite different dining custom. This was one that was presently to make the town notable, or notorious (depending on how one viewed such matters) all over the nation. For, as stated earlier, all three had on their upper floors rows of small dining cubicles, each boasting, besides a table, a couch standing against one wall and a door that could be locked from the inside.

For the convenience of those making use of such facilities, each resort had what was euphemistically termed a carriage entrance, which was on a side street and opened on a stairway that led directly upstairs. Thus male patrons and their companions of the evening—who usually arrived in hacks with the shades discreetly drawn—could reach their hideaways without having to pass through the crowded dining room on the street level.

It was these well-patronized upstairs retreats at the Poodle Dog, the Maison Riche, and the Maison Dorée that—more even than the Barbary Coast honky-tonks and its booming tenderloin districts—gained for the town its reputation as "the Paris of America." Yet while that aspect of the restaurants was deplored by reputable citizens, and roundly denounced from every pulpit, the food served was of such excellence that few even of the most censorious could bring themselves to forego the pleasure of dining there. Happily, a compromise was reached, one that must have been acceptable to all, for it remained in force for many years. This was simplicity itself: a line of demarcation was drawn dividing the establishments into two separate and distinct parts. By that device, the main dining rooms on the ground floor came to be regarded as uncontaminated, with only the upstairs areas off bounds to the respectable.

The popularity, and prosperity, of the original "big three" encouraged others to enter the field, and by the mid-1890s the town had a dozen or more French cafés. Most of these catered to those who, while relishing the excellence of the food they served, could not afford the prices charged at the Poodle Dog, the Maison Riche, and the Maison Dorée. These less expensive resorts were scattered throughout the downtown area, mostly on the side streets off Kearny, Montgomery, and Sansome, and in the triangle formed by Market, Geary, and Powell. There on long, family-style tables, covered with oilcloth, were served meals consisting of soup, fish, entree, and salad, and winding up with fruit, cheese, and cups of bitter black coffee, all prepared in a manner to delight the most discriminating, and at a cost of thirty-five to fifty cents, which always included a pint of passable California wine.

Long one of the most popular of these was the Hotel de France, which occupied an ornate former residence on the rise of California Street between Kearny and Dupont. On entering it from the sidewalk one stepped down a short flight of stairs, crossed a little wooden bridge, and thus gained what had once been the front parlor. This had been converted into a reasonable likeness of a French bistro, complete with zinc bar, and presided over by a buxom, bemustached barmaid in severe black dress. The place boasted two dining rooms. One, across the hall from the bar, was a small chamber fitted up with individual tables with white cloths; this was mainly patronized by those with a taste for elegance and a desire for a certain amount of privacy.

Regular patrons, however, would have none of this. They made their way to the big room in the rear, which was crowded with long tables, down the center of each of which were spaced bowls of fruit, platters of celery, radishes, and young onions, and long loaves of crisp, new-baked French bread.

The meal itself, which varied little from month to month or year to year, started off with the patron ladling out a dish of thick cabbage soup from steaming tureens brought in from the kitchen. This was followed by a fish course, sand dabs or sole or smelt fried to a rich brown and covered with a savory sauce that was one of the specialties of the house. Next came the entree: chicken on Sundays and on other days either roast or boiled beef. These last were not served in individual portions; instead, the huge cuts were brought in on platters, along with dishes of vegetables, and each diner carved off a piece to his liking. Then came bowls of salad—always mixed by Louis, the owner, who scorned to use any but olive oil in the process—and the repast ended by each customer helping himself to the bountiful supply of fruit—apples, oranges, peaches, pears, or grapes—in the center of the table.

And what was the cost of this banquet—including, of course, a pint of new but palatable red wine? For years it had been fifteen cents on weekdays and two bits on Sundays.

By the time the 1890s arrived, however, inflation had got in its work and the tariffs had soared to twenty-five cents during the week and thirty-five on the Sabbath. There were, however, those who stoutly maintained that the Hotel de France's bountiful, and well-prepared, meals were well worth even that advanced price.

In the area a bit farther to the north and east, impinging on the town's Bohemian quarter, were a group of other restaurants where the hungry painter, sculptor, musician, or scribbler could get a thoroughly satisfactory meal, both as regards quantity and quality, for a maximum of twenty-five cents. One of the most frequented of these was the Tour Eiffel. This long stood at the corner of Montgomery and Jackson, and hence was convenient to the studios in the outmoded brick and wooden buildings on these and neighboring streets. Another favorite was the Brooklyn Hotel, a bit farther afield on the 200 block on Bush Street, the proprietor of which, Charles Montgomery, long advertised two-bit dinners and, moreover, provided varied and bountiful meals, well-cooked and tastefully served.

Resorts such as these were the usual dining places for the town's artistic set during periods when their finances were low—which in a majority of cases was virtually all the time. When, however, by the sale of a painting, a story, or some other stroke of luck, one found himself in funds and wished to celebrate his windfall, there was no lack of more pretentious cafés to which he might go. These ranged from Sanguinetti's, Coppa's, Luchetti's, and other "four-bit houses" to such renowned establishments as the original French "big three," plus the Fly Trap, the Pup, and Marchand's, spiraling upward in price until it reached its zenith in the world-famous dining room of Colonel Kirkpatrick's Palace Hotel.

II.

One North Beach restaurant much frequented by the literati throughout the 1890s was Luna's, which specialized in tamales, enchiladas, tortillas, and other fiery-hot delicacies from south of the border. The place was off the main-traveled streets and the uninitiated often had trouble finding it. For, wrote Frank Norris, "Luna's Mexican restaurant has no address. It is on no particular street, at no particular corner, even its habitués, its most enthusiastic devotees, are unable to locate it upon demand. . . . It is 'over there in the quarter,' 'not far from the cathedral there.' One could find it if one started out with that intent; but to direct another there —no, that is out of the question. It *can* be reached by following the alleys of Chinatown. You will come out of the last alley—the one where the slave girls are—upon the edge of the Mexican quarter, and by going ahead for a block or two, and by keeping a sharp lookout to the right and left you will hit upon it. It is always to be searched for. Always to be discovered."

That means of finding Luna's seems to have been ample in the free-and-easy 1890s, for the place was frequented not only by the town's considerable Spanish and Mexican population but by its artists and writers. For the benefit of a later and more literal-minded age, however, it should be stated that Luna's stood at the corner of Vallejo and Dupont streets (now Grant Avenue), on the lower slope of Telegraph Hill. Housed in a little wooden dwelling that had been built in the 1850s, it had undergone virtually no structural changes on being taken over for commercial uses; consequently, its patrons had the feeling that they were dining in a private home.

To reach the dining room one passed through a prim Victorian parlor, where the proprietress was usually to be found seated in the bay window busily engaged in sewing or some other domestic chore. There was, however, one concession to merchandising in that center of domesticity. For against one wall was a showcase in which was displayed a stock of Mexican goods: gaily painted pottery, bright-colored scarves, handkerchiefs and neckties, plus a tray or two of silver rings, pins, and other trinkets to tempt diners passing to and from the room beyond.

That chamber, complete with Nottingham lace curtains at its windows, contained about a dozen tables, each with a white-and-red-checked cloth and an assortment of bottles and bowls containing relishes and sauces, all extremely hot. The table d'hôte "Supper Mexican"—fifty cents on weekdays, seventy-five cents on Sundays—customarily began with tiny Mexican sausages and several varieties of marinated pickles, proceeded through soup, an enchilada, chile con carne, chiles rellenos—peppers stuffed with cheese—frijoles fritas, and for dessert, a concoction of egg yolks, cinnamon, raisins, and nuts enclosed in a flaky crust and baked to a rich brown. This last was known to patrons as a "sweet tamale."

Presiding over the dining room was the incomparable Riccardo, a giant of a man whose velvet jacket, red sash, and fierce black mustache gave him the look of a brigand, an effect that was enhanced by the fact that one eye was missing and he wore a black patch over the empty socket. Despite his bloodthirsty appearance, however, Riccardo was a deft and solicitous waiter and a prime favorite with the regular diners. Among the most faithful of these was Norris, then in his twenties and subeditor of the *Wave*, to which he each week contributed an article on some phase of the life of the city or a bit of fiction. His real ambition, however, was to write realistic novels in the manner of his admired Emile Zola.

Young Norris was then paying court to the pretty nineteen-year-old girl whom he presently married, and their Sunday afternoon rambles about the town usually ended with "Supper Mexican" at Luna's. His novel, *Blix,* published in 1899, was largely a fictionized version of their romance, and some of the most entertaining chapters of that high-spirited tale are laid at Luna's, which he described as "a quiet little old fashioned place . . . respectable as a tomb."

The two young people of the story, Condy Rivers and Blix, were one evening reading the "Personals" in a local newspaper—mostly advertisements of lonely men and women seeking acquaintance with members of the opposite sex, "object matrimony." One ad, that of a woman who signed herself K.D.B., was so demurely phrased as to stir the interest of the pair, and they amused themselves by choosing from the others one they thought would make her a suitable mate. Having considered and rejected a number of other would-be bridegrooms, their choice finally fell to one signed "Captain Jack," who described himself as a retired sea captain, "twenty-nine, sober and industrious."

Suddenly Condy and Blix had what at the time seemed to them a brilliant idea: to bring the pair together by writing each a letter purportedly coming from the other, both suggesting a meeting at Luna's at seven on the following Monday evening, and the lady proposing that each wear a white marguerite as a means of identification. The letters were duly written and mailed and on the appointed evening the conspirators made their way to the restaurant a little ahead of the scheduled time, intent on witnessing the meeting. There were, of course, unlooked-for complications. For on entering the dining room they found seated there not one but **two** men, each sporting a white marguerite in his buttonhole.

The problem confronting Condy and Blix was to find out which of this pair was the authentic Captain Jack and, having done so, to hit on means of promptly getting rid of the interloper, for the lady, K.D.B., was expected at any moment. The first of these tasks the resourceful duo accomplished in the following manner: On the wall was a chromo depicting a schooner-rigged ship sailing on an emerald sea. In a voice that could be heard by the others, Blix asked her companion what manner of ship it was, and Condy in his most authoritative tone called it a brigantine, meanwhile watching the others closely to observe their reaction to that misinformation. One —and to their mind the less prepossessing of the two—showed no interest in the conversation; the other, however, expressed his contempt at Condy's ignorance of things maritime by an audible snort.

Thus half of the problem was solved. There remained, however, the matter of getting rid of the interloper. In their dilemma the two thought fast, and it was Blix who came up with the answer. Why not, she whispered, send a telegram to the unwanted diner, one that would cause him to flee at once? The message was duly written, and Condy—having learned the other's initials by stealing a glimpse inside his hat—hurried to the nearest telegraph office. Soon a messenger boy appeared, conferred briefly with Riccardo, who took the envelope over to the man, saying: "I guess this is for you, Mr. Adams." The other tore it open, read and reread the message, meanwhile frowning furiously. "His 'Supper Mexican,' " the account continues, "remained untasted before him; Condy and Blix heard him breathing hard . . . All at once . . . he rose, seized his hat, jammed it over his ears, slapped a half-dollar upon the table, and strode from the restaurant." The message that caused his precipitate retreat read: "All is discovered. Fly at once."

The troubles of the matchmakers, however, were not yet over. For when K.D.B. presently appeared—a small, composed, competent-appearing young woman who "looked like a servant girl of the better sort"—Captain Jack was seized by panic and hastily removed the flower from his lapel. "Hitherto," commented the narrator, "he had acted the role of a sane and sensible gentleman . . . master of himself and of the situation. The entrance of K.D.B. had evidently reduced him to a semi-idiotic condition . . . He frowned terribly at trifling articles in the corners of the room. He cleared his throat until the glassware trembled. He pulled at his mustache . . ." And all the while K.D.B. was "calmly sitting in her corner picking daintily at her fish," seemingly unaware of the captain's discomposure.

When a quarter hour had passed with no signs of recognition on the part of either, it dawned on Condy and Blix that they themselves were the reason for the impasse. "They'll never meet so long as we're here," whispered Condy. "Let's go and give 'em a chance." But Blix had set her heart on seeing the outcome of their little scheme, and presently they hit on a plan that would make this possible. They paid their bill and took their leave, but Condy, pretending absent-mindedness, left his walking stick behind. "They walked as far as the cathedral, listened for a moment to the bell striking the hour of eight," then hurried back and reclaimed his property.

"On the curb outside," Norris's account concludes, "Condy and Blix shook hands . . . In the back room, seated at the same table, a bunch of wilted marguerites between them, they had seen their 'matrimonial objects' conferring earnestly, absorbed in the business of getting acquainted."

III.

It was, however, not Luna's but a quite different restaurant in another part of North Beach that has come to be most closely identified with the Bohemian life of the town during that period. This was Coppa's, which at the turn of the century and for a half dozen years thereafter occupied a narrow, high-ceilinged room in the Montgomery Block at the corner of Montgomery and Merchant. Presided over by Giuseppe ("Pop") Coppa—a rotund and genial product of northern Italy, complete with black skullcap and flowing mustache—the place had a bar in front, some twenty tables ranged along its walls and down the middle, with a kitchen, plus a second room to take care of the overflow, in the rear.

Before he opened his Montgomery Street resort, Coppa had served as cook in a number of leading hotels and restaurants, among the latter Martinelli's and the Poodle Dog. Then he had launched into business on his own, first in a tiny place on a North Beach alley, and a few years later—his *pastas* and good country wine having found favor with residents of the area—he had moved to larger quarters in the Montgomery Block.

Not only did his regular customers follow him to the new location, but a sprinkling of artists and writers who lived close by soon formed the habit of partaking of his copious and reasonably priced dinners: a heaping plate of spaghetti, a half loaf of crisp Italian bread, and a pint of wine, all for twenty-five cents.

It was not Coppa's food, however, excellent and cheap as it was, that gave the place the renown it presently came to enjoy. For somewhere in the owner's expansive person lurked the ambition to become a painter, and although it was not until his later years that he took up the hobby, he meantime had a feeling of kinship with those artists and writers and other Bohemians who had begun frequenting his café. His manifest admiration was, of course, flattering to the latter, but what really won their hearts was the fact that during their periods of financial stress he good-naturedly permitted them to sign chits for their meals, thus tiding them over until the sale of a picture or story put them in funds again.

It was primarily to show their appreciation of this that a group of regular customers soon embarked on a project that was destined to give Coppa's an honored place in the annals of the bayside Bohemia. This came about in the following manner: In 1903 or thereabouts, the walls of his establishment having grown dingy, Coppa one day had them repapered. In doing so, however, he failed to consult his artist friends and patrons. The result was that the color he had selected offended the sensibilities of the group, one of whom described it as "a particularly violent shade of red." When they gathered at their usual table that evening they not only made known their distress to Coppa but offered themselves to do a redecorating job on the walls, contributing their time and talents free.

Coppa's response to this proposal was less than enthusiastic. His bright crimson walls seemed to him the height of elegance, and besides, there was no telling what sort of decorations these uninhibited artists might have in mind. At length, however, his consent was reluctantly given, and on the following Sunday—Coppa's being closed on that day—the group went to work. Placing tables one on another to form insecure platforms, and fortified with sandwiches and jugs of Napa wine their host had set out for them, they began sketching their designs in bright-colored chalks against the red background.

Three men tried their hands at the project that first Sunday. Porter Garnett, working on the north wall, produced a ferocious-looking lobster, some five feet tall, standing rampant on an island labeled Bohemia. Robert Aitken, later a sculptor of note, whose San Francisco productions include the Dewey Monument in Union Square, drew two amiable-appearing nudes, while the third member, Perry Newberry, soon to become unofficial "mayor" of Carmel, added his bit.

Next Sunday the work continued. Warming to his task, Garnett drew, a foot or two below the ceiling, a frieze enclosed in a decorative border, its purpose being, in his words, "to draw the various elements of the composition together." On this border were lettered the names of those, past and present, whom the group considered eligible for inclusion in Bohemia's Hall of Fame. The list of those so honored was a curious one, for side by side with Rabelais, Dante, and Sappho, were the names of the participating artists, plus certain local writers and a number of ladies whom the painters currently admired. Two of the latter bore the names Buttski and Isabel I, Buttski being a local dramatist, Bertha Brubaker, whom Newberry later married, and Isabel was Isabel Fraser, a writer of Sunday features for young Hearst's *Examiner*. A third member of this company was Maisie, the group's name for another girl journalist, Mary Edith Griswold, then on the staff of the *Chronicle*.

Extending about the room just above that all-inclusive Hall of Fame was a line of stalking black cats, the handiwork of "Marty" Martinez. That flamboyant Mexican artist was recently back from six years in the Paris ateliers, his corduroy coat, baggy trousers, black velvet beret, and flowing red tie making him easily the most colorful figure of the group.

The Hall of Fame and Marty's procession of cats, were,

however, but a frame enclosing as odd an assortment of drawings as the good burghers of San Francisco had ever gazed on. For during the next several months the work went on until in the end every foot of wall space on three sides of the room was covered. The artists did not hesitate to include in their compositions caricatures both of themselves and their cronies. Thus it became a favorite pastime of the Philistines, who were presently appearing in numbers each night, to try to identify the artists at the long central table with their likenesses on the walls.

Among those depicted, besides Garnett, Aitken, and Newberry, were Gelett Burgess—whose contribution was a series of his odd-looking creatures with oversized heads and bodies that defied all the rules of anatomy—Martinez, swarthy-faced, with an unruly mop of black hair; George Sterling, lean-faced and gaunt (as became a poet) with a laurel wreath, slightly askew, on his head, and Maynard Dixon, decked out in cowboy boots, tight pants, and, on his elongated head, a huge ten-gallon hat.

Farther down the crowded north wall was a group of figures designed both to amuse the artists and bewilder the uninitiated. These included a benign-looking devil toasting one cloven foot among the coals of a fire while holding a fishing pole at the end of which was a prodigious fish. Nearby was a singularly lecherous-appearing satyr touching champagne glasses with a comely maiden whose nakedness was partially concealed behind the trunk of a tree. As a means of incorporating Coppa's big wall clock into the composition, Father Time was depicted, lying flat on his back, his skinny legs extending upward to support the clock, at the same time balancing on the finger of one hand an hourglass and on the other a bottle of wine.

With such conceits, each seemingly more preposterous than

its neighbor, Papa Coppa's entire wall space was covered. For those areas not occupied by humans, animals, or scenery were given over to scrolls and plaques on which were inscribed—in English, Latin, Hebrew, and medieval French—quotations from the philosophers, ancient and modern, expressing sentiments deemed appropriate to grace the walls of Bohemia. These for the most part were selected and inscribed by the erudite Garnett.

Even more than the pictures themselves, these recondite inscriptions served to baffle the slummers, who by then made up the most numerous, and profitable, of Coppa's customers. Considering the cryptic nature of most of these writings, one can sympathize with the pair of uptown visitors depicted in one of the drawings: a lady wearing a fashionable ostrich plume on her hat seated opposite her bald-headed escort, a bottle of champagne on the table between them. Both are staring at a neighboring table, at which sit a group of posturing, long-haired artists. "Freaks!" observes the lady, and her companion replies: "Yes, artists!"

Coppa's murals and the enigma they presented to the townspeople proved an unexpected stroke of good fortune to the genial restaurateur. For from the day of their completion Coppa's fame spread throughout the city and farther afield, and thereafter—until the fire of 1906 ended the fun—his every table was nightly filled to capacity. Later, striving to repeat that success, he opened other restaurants in the rebuilt downtown area, decorating each in a manner reminiscent of his old Montgomery Street quarters. But the new drawings somehow seemed to lack the spontaneity and uninhibited drollery of the old. Or perhaps it was merely that times had changed and the original group of artists and scribblers who had given the old place its authentic Bohemian atmosphere had scattered to the four winds. At any rate, in his later ventures he was never able to recapture the old, carefree spirit, and in the late 1930s—he being then close to eighty—Papa Coppa retired permanently from the field.

One leading figure of the original Coppa group was Porter Garnett, connoisseur of art and elegant living and an authority on the works of the more recondite writers and painters and musicians of the day, both at home and abroad. Not only was young Garnett an authentic bon vivant but—what was equally important—he looked the part. Small of stature and slightly built, he made up for his lack of bulk by decking himself out in the height of fashion, his London-made suits and hats and topcoats possessing an elegance rivaled only by those of his friend and contemporary, Frank Norris.

Garnett came naturally by his liking for sartorial splendor. San Francisco-born and the son of a prosperous merchant, it was his custom as a child to mount his pony and accompany his mother's carriage on shopping trips downtown, his miniature riding habit correct to the last detail. On these tours he waited, erect and motionless, on his mount outside, seemingly oblivious to the crowd of onlookers who always gathered about, until his mother reappeared. It is recorded that on one occasion when he had thus stationed himself before the Lace House, the owner of that fashionable establishment, Raphael Weill, came out and, taking the bridle, gravely led pony and rider on a tour of the premises, passing up one aisle and down the next until the entire ground floor had been covered.

As a young man Garnett had a dilettante's interest in many fields of art and a considerable proficiency in two, namely, writing and drawing. He was an occasional contributor of verse and prose to the more advanced of the local journals, and his stylized, vaguely Beardsleyesque drawings were widely admired. Garnett's real contribution to the artistic life of the town—and it was a considerable one—lay, however, in his close friendship with the group of young writers and painters then just coming to the fore, and in his role as arbiter of *fin de siècle* elegance and good taste, the influence he exerted on their work.

It was not until well after the turn of the century that Garnett found his true vocation—not in writing or drawing but in the field of printing. To this he devoted the last two decades of his life, first as director of typography in San Francisco shops and later at his celebrated Laboratory Press on the campus of Carnegie Tech at Pittsburgh. He died in 1951 at the age of eighty.

IV.

Throughout the 1890s the town abounded in picturesque eating places to which residents and tourists alike journeyed in quest not only of excellent food but of quaint or bizarre surroundings. One such was Warner's Cobweb Palace, a ramshackle structure perched precariously on Meiggs's Wharf, which extended out into the bay from North Beach.

Presided over by an eccentric ex-sailor named Abe Warner, the resort was no more conventional than its owner. Its three rooms were cluttered with an assortment of curios gathered from all points of the compass: bolos and warclubs from the South Sea Islands, a totem pole and Eskimo canoe from the far north, Chinese and Japanese masks and screens and porcelains, graven images from the ruined temples of the Aztecs, and much else, all stacked one on the other without rhyme or reason and thickly covered with many years' accumulation of grime and cobwebs.

This, however, was not all. For in addition to these relics

the place boasted a considerable menagerie. Cages containing a brace of California cinnamon bears and half a dozen monkeys stood outside the door, while assorted dogs and cats, plus a bevy of magpies, parakeets, and other shrill-voiced birds had the run of the place and raised a continual din.

As befitted its location above the waters of the bay, the Cobweb Palace served only sea food, the specialties of the house being clam chowder—which was excellent—cracked crab, and mussels Bordelaise. The true fame of the establish-ment, however, rested not on any of these but on the quality of the drinks served at its tiny bar. This, an unprepossessing room which could be reached only by picking one's way through the litter of the first two chambers, offered what, in the opinion of the town's connoisseurs, was as complete an assortment of rare, imported wines, brandies, and liquors as could be found anywhere. For Warner disdained to set before his patrons anything but the finest, pointing out that those who lacked discrimination in such matters could find ample cheap rum, gin, and whiskey at any corner saloon. The conse-quence was that all through the 1890s it was the habit of the local bon vivants, following an ample dinner at one or another of the downtown cafés, to hail a cab, drive out to the North Beach resort, and top off the evening by sipping one of Warner's mellow French brandies.

For all through that period the townspeople were highly food-, and drink-, conscious and they regularly visited first one and then another of a dozen different restaurants and bars in order to enjoy the specialties of the house: oysters Kirkpatrick at the Palace, the potent pisco punch served by Duncan Nichol at the Bank Exchange, and numerous others.

In any catalogue of the dishes that made the town a gourmet's Elysium during those years a place near the top of the list would surely be accorded chicken portola, long the chef-d'oeuvre of Coppa's. Although this creation—its price was $1.75 per serving—was normally beyond the reach of the artists and poets and journalists who frequented the place, on those rare occasions when they found themselves in funds there was but one proper way for them to celebrate: Papa Coppa was grandly ordered to bring forth his masterpiece. This, however, was at best an infrequent occurrence, and for the most part chicken portola graced the tables of prosperous citizens from farther uptown.

Be that as it may, few who partook of the delicacy failed to pronounce it a rare gastronomic treat. As a first step in preparing it, the top of a coconut was sawed off and most of the fruit scooped out. Into it was then inserted a dismembered spring chicken, swimming in a sauce composed of shredded coconut, onions, fresh corn, tomatoes, chopped green peppers, diced bacon fried in olive oil, and a variety of condiments. Finally, the top was replaced and sealed down with a paste and the whole placed in a pan of water and baked for an hour, with frequent bastings. When cooked to a turn, the coconuts—one to each diner—were brought to the table piping-hot, and when the waiter removed the tops, the savory ingredients within filled the room with a mouth-watering aroma. Without exception, those who were privileged to taste the concoction pronounced it "fit for a king."

In that less complex age democracy was the byword among all segments of the population. The plutocrat was on easy terms with the cabby who daily drove him from his turreted Nob Hill castle to his downtown office, the two addressing each other by their first names and with no feeling of condescension on the part of either. Those who rode the cable cars knew by name every gripman and conductor on the line they patronized, and it was no uncommon sight to see housewives hail the cars in the residential streets and give the conductor a message—written or oral—for delivery to her husband at an office or store at the other end of the line.

Thus during the mid-1890s, when the nurses at the newly established French Hospital on outer Point Lobos Avenue planned a feast on coming off duty at midnight, they gave the carman a dollar, with instructions to buy them an oyster loaf. That concoction, a favorite late-evening snack for San Franciscans of all degrees, was merely a loaf of fresh-baked French bread that had been sliced lengthwise, part of its insides scooped out, the aperture filled with several dozen fried oysters, and the top, liberally buttered, replaced. Having left the order at an all-night café at the corner of Geary and Polk on his way downtown, the conductor would pick it up on his return trip and, stowing it carefully on top of the kerosene lamp at the front end of his dummy, deliver it piping-hot to the nurse on duty at the desk.

V.

While by the end of the 1890s the quality of the food served by a number of the town's leading restaurants had gained them a considerable renown all over the country, it was not such resorts that most impressed those newcomers who considered themselves authorities on the pleasures of the table. No, what remained longest in memory—at least in the memory of male visitors—was something quite different; namely, the unsurpassed size and variety of the free lunches provided to comers at its leading bars.

That San Francisco's pre-eminence in that regard was justly earned becomes clear when one considers the viands daily set forth to tempt the appetites of patrons of a single resort, this one being Charley Newman's Yellowstone Bar on Montgomery Street. For at its counter, which extended the entire length of the long room, and was presided over by a corps of white-clad Chinese waiters, were to be found at all times such delicacies as Camembert, Brie, Gorgonzola, Limburger, and half a dozen other cheeses, caviar, guava sandwiches, sweetbreads on toast, alligator pear salad with nasturtium leaves, diamond-back terrapin Maryland, Virginia ham baked in French brandy, roast venison, clams fried in chopped olives and corn meal, shrimps in jellied crème de menthe, and—for those with less exotic tastes—roast beef, pork, lamb, and corned beef and cabbage.

Incredible as it sounds in the present Spartan era, when a bowl of pretzels or salted peanuts constitutes about all in the way of provender laid out at our cocktail bars, this bountiful offering was by no means unique. The Yellowstone's menu was, in fact, looked on as strictly run-of-the-mill; half a dozen other resorts on Montgomery, Kearny, Market, and intersecting streets served lunches as elaborate or more so. Each had its specialties, a fact well known to those who daily followed the cocktail route: oysters on the half shell at the Palace Bar, frog legs poulette at the Occidental, dove pie with mushrooms at Rome Harris's place at Kearny and Bush, lobster Newburg at the Hoffman House, and, at the Reception, crab legs in cream sauce with sherry.

Out-of-towners never ceased to marvel that these elaborate feasts were served to all comers, the man whose only purchase was a five-cent schooner of beer being no less welcome than the most prodigal spenders. To be sure, at some of the resorts a porter was charged with spotting those who patronized the lunch counters without crossing to the bar for a spot of liquid refreshment, and these, if their visits grew too frequent, were politely advised to take their patronage elsewhere. However, that rule was but laxly enforced at a majority of the saloons—at some not at all—and it is of record that many frugal residents daily made the rounds and thus fared very well at no cost whatever. Most of these free-loaders were, of course, known, but it was an easygoing, liberal age and the owners took the view that they were potential customers who chanced to be temporarily down in their luck.

The décor of many of these establishments was no less elaborate than their free lunches. Even in an age not noted for austerity in such matters, San Francisco's barrooms set new standards of opulence. Each owner strove to outdo his competitors in the elegance of his premises, and if there existed in any of them a square foot of space that had not been embellished within an inch of its life, it must have been due to an oversight.

Floors were commonly of tile or marble, laid in intricate patterns, and it was a rare ceiling that was not strewn with plaster nymphs and satyrs in bas-relief. The bars themselves were usually of mahogany or rosewood, their tops and richly carved sides polished until they shone like mirrors, while on the wall behind was an impressive array of bottled goods, interspersed with glasses of many sizes and shapes ranged in tall, glistening pyramids.

Although each strove for a certain individuality in matters of decoration, one element was common to all, for no San Francisco bar of the 1890s, however unpretentious, was considered properly fitted out without at least a few works of art gracing its walls. In the neighborhood resorts thickly strewn throughout the residential districts, and the East Street grogshops serving waterfront workers, the owners catered to the aesthetic sense of their patrons by a display of colored lithographs, most of them advertising products dispensed at the bar, the most popular being "Custer's Last Stand."

The more sophisticated clientele of the big downtown resorts were, however, exposed to a different variety of art; namely, oil paintings of generous size and realistic treatment. These, as their owners proudly pointed out, were all originals, most of them executed by a group of local artists who specialized in work of that sort, the most widely known of whom was A. D. Cooper. The fact that the subjects pictured were invariably nudes—it being well recognized that barroom critics had no interest in landscapes—lent a certain sameness to these displays, but no one seemed to mind. Besides, the artists were able to lend diversity to their canvases by depicting the ladies in a wide variety of poses.

Thus while a majority of the works showed the subjects in more or less conventional postures—reclining at ease on a bearskin was a particular favorite—not a few displayed considerably more imagination. Susanna and the Elders was frequently done, as was also a scene that depicted a Numidian slave girl being auctioned off to a group of highly lascivious-appearing Arab sheiks. Yet another was a stately blond maiden from northern climes marching, shackled but proud, among a file of Caesar's returning legions, the columns of the Roman Forum visible in the background.

That such representations of historical scenes were closely studied by the town's drinkers is evidenced by the fact that Mark Twain, during his few months' stay in the mid-1860s, triumphantly announced that he had discovered a glaring anachronism in one such canvas. This treated of a Biblical theme: a buxom, scantily clad Delilah deftly shearing off the locks of the sleeping Samson. Twain's contention was that the shears she was using were of a type that did not come into use until some twenty centuries later.

Paintings of plump nudes—for, like landscapes, maidens without plenty of flesh on their bones found little favor with

the town's serious drinkers—adorned the walls of every barroom of any claim to elegance, as necessary a part of the
equipment as the traditional brass rail and the row of big
cuspidors spaced at intervals down the length of the room.
However, one resort, on Pine Street, a few doors above Montgomery, outshone its competitors by covering every foot of
wall space with a gallery of such ladies, crowded as closely
together as the frames would permit.

Terming itself the Palace of Art, this establishment not
only became one of the regular stops on the cocktail route
but was the spot, according to one observer, where the pilgrims dawdled over their drinks far longer than elsewhere.
To be sure, this same critic thought little of the artistic merit
of the works displayed there, terming them "framed acres of
trash." This was, however, an opinion not shared by a majority of the town's males, few of whom, when showing strangers
the sights of the town, failed to include the Palace of Art in
their itinerary.

CHAPTER 5

A Gallery of Folk Heroes

I.

From its earliest days San Francisco had been a good theater town, its amusement-starved first residents nightly crowding the pioneer playhouses and giving an uproarious welcome to their favorites—who, incidentally, included a goodly number of troupers then at the beginning of their careers who went on to make distinguished names for themselves on the American stage.

During the final years of the century the city continued to maintain this well-established tradition. Indeed, throughout the 1890s there were those who contended that San Francisco had more theaters, and supported them more liberally, than any other city in the country. There is, moreover, some evidence that this was no idle boast. Among show people it was everywhere looked on as one of the bright spots of the nation, a town where, provided only that their offerings were entertaining and the casts reasonably proficient, road companies could look forward to long and profitable runs.

It was, however, not these traveling troupes that provided

local playgoers with their staple dramatic fare. For one thing, such companies appeared only at intervals, and thousands of residents were in the habit of taking in at least one show a week. The result was that there were generally two or three— and sometimes as many as half a dozen—stock companies playing simultaneously, their offerings ranging from ten–twenty–thirty-cent melodrama on through vaudeville, minstrel shows, standard plays and operettas, to grand opera itself.

Among the most popular houses of the period were those of Walter Morosco. Having begun to produce his lurid melodramas—at a top of twenty cents—in a hall above a livery stable at Third and Howard streets, he in 1894 took over the big, barnlike Grand Opera House on Mission Street. This he packed to the doors every night for the next five years, presenting such spectacles as *The Great Diamond Robbery, The Wages of Sin,* and others of like nature. It is of interest to know that among those appearing in these lurid dramas were two youths who were destined to go far in the theatrical world: Theodore Roberts, actor, and William A. Brady, producer.

Among other well-patronized houses were the Bush Street Theater and the California. The last named, put up in the late 1860s by the flamboyant local banker, William C. Ralston, was long hailed as the most luxuriously appointed playhouse in the country. Its grand opening on the night of January 18, 1869, was recalled with respect for a generation after. For the wealth and beauty of the town had crowded its ground floor and boxes, comanagers Lawrence Barrett and John McCullough had acted as hosts, and an admired local poet, one F. Bret Harte, had read a six-stanza poem he had composed for the occasion.

During the next twenty years, under the management first of Barrett and McCullough and later of Barton Hill, a long succession of illustrious mimes trod its boards. The list included, besides Barrett and McCullough, Edwin Booth, Mrs. Judah, Joseph Jefferson, Mary Anderson, Henry Montague, Helena Modjeska, James O'Neill, E. A. and E. H. Southern, the indestructible Lotta Crabtree, and a host of others. When, following the opening of the Baldwin and other houses farther uptown, patronage at the California began to fall off, the ornate old structure was razed. It was, however, presently replaced by another, the New California. This was within the walls of a big hotel built by Mrs. Kate MacDonough, a sister of bonanza king William S. O'Brien. It, along with the entire central part of the city, went up in smoke in 1906.

The Bush Street Theater, originally called the Alhambra, was another prime favorite throughout most of the 1890s. Under the management of Mike Leavitt, himself a veteran end man of touring minstrel shows, the house went in for a more bawdy type of entertainment than its competitors, introducing such novelties as can-can dancers, double-entendre jokes and songs, and troupes of buxom, scantily clad chorus girls. While these devices caused business to boom at the box office, they frequently brought Leavitt and his performers into difficulties with the morals squad of the local police department.

On one such occasion, when a troupe billed as "Mme. D'Est's Blondes, Red Stocking and Blue Garter Minstrels" was entertaining the populace, the entire company was hauled into court on a charge of indecency. The defendants demanded a jury trial and their attorney insisted that the jurors witness the show. This strategy, however, failed to work out as planned. For notwithstanding the prosecution's charge that the show had been drastically cleaned up for that one performance, the jurors returned a verdict of guilty and the judge levied a substantial fine.

Despite such brushes with the law, however, the Bush Street remained one of the town's leading playhouses through most of the 1890s. Although by then minstrel shows were fast becoming passé, the black-faced comedians continued to have a loyal following there as well as at several other local houses. One perennial favorite was Billy Emerson, who had broken into show business with manager Leavitt years earlier. Emerson's California Minstrels rarely failed to play to crowded houses, San Franciscans taking a special delight in his barbed comments on matters of current local interest, particularly on the behavior of the town's politicians.

Like the other stock companies, Emerson's minstrels proved an excellent training ground for ambitious beginners. In the early 1880s one of his black-faced crew was a young Irish tenor named Chauncey Olcott; a year or two later another tyro, twenty-four-year-old Nat Goodwin, there began his rise to fame, fortune, and a succession of pretty wives. At the Bush Street, too, San Franciscans got their first delighted glimpses of a beginner named Helen Leonard who, as Lillian Russell, was to become a reigning queen of musical comedy.

As the century drew toward its close, other names were added to the galaxy of stars who got their starts in the theater-mad town. Among them—to name but a few—were Florence Roberts and Bert Lytell, who were presently playing leads in stock at the Alcazar on O'Farrell Street; Nance O'Neill, an Oakland girl who made her debut at the same house in 1893; Blanche Bates, daughter of the old-time troupers Mr. and Mrs. F. M. Bates, and a bit player named Frank Bacon, who came from San Jose and who years later was to win lasting renown for his role in *Lightnin'*.

Yet another local youth who was captivated by the lure of the footlights was David Warfield. Warfield's theatrical career, which eventually carried him to the heights, began modestly enough, as a vender of candy and peanuts who during intermissions passed up and down the aisles of the old California hawking his wares. Later he served as an usher, both at the California and at the Wigwam, an early-day vaudeville house. All the while, however, his real interest lay backstage, and from time to time he was pressed into service as a super at one or another of the local houses, carrying a spear in mob scenes or stepping on briefly as messenger boy or servant.

It was not until 1889, when he was twenty-three, that Warfield was given his first speaking part, that of a minor character in the then popular farce, *The Ticket of Leave Man.* From that time on, however, his progress was rapid. For he presently attracted the attention of a fellow townsman, David Belasco, and soon after Belasco moved on to New York he summoned the other to join him. The rest is theatrical history. On the lookout for a part suited to his young protégé's style of acting, Belasco at length found exactly what he wanted in Charles Klein's *The Auctioneer.* In this Warfield played the title role for three years, from 1900 to 1903, thereby winning himself a place as one of the best-loved actors of his generation.

This was followed in 1904 by another Klein play, *The Music Master,* in which, as Herr Anton von Berwig, Warfield scored an even greater success. During the next decade he appeared in a succession of other Belasco productions—*The Grand Army Man* and *The Return of Peter Grimm* among them—always playing the kindly, crotchety, humorous characters that had first won him acclaim in *The Auctioneer.*

On his occasional returns to San Francisco he never failed

to play to packed houses. Once, in the mid-1890s, when it was announced that he would appear as Shylock in *The Merchant of Venice,* a local rabbi sought him out and urged him not to essay that role, arguing that to do so would add fuel to the prejudice against the Jews, which was already strong in some quarters. Politely but firmly Warfield rejected the other's plea. Instead, he urged his caller to withhold judgment until he could observe the audience's reaction. The rabbi followed that advice, and on the opening night Warfield's performance was a masterly one. He was an intensely human Shylock, the pathetic victim of the age-long oppression of his people, and so convincingly portrayed that at the fall of the curtain the rabbi joined in the tremendous ovation accorded him.

II.

The townspeople kept a sharp eye on what was happening throughout the theatrical world, and when new plays, or players, began to win plaudits elsewhere, a clamor at once arose to have them brought out for the approval—or, frequently, the disapproval—of local audiences. The town's managers were well aware of this, and often went to considerable lengths to satisfy it. Thus, if a new play was packing them in on Broadway, not many weeks would pass before San Franciscans had an opportunity to witness it, played either by a road show or one of the local stock companies.

Few of these productions returned any profit to their authors or original producers, for in those days copyright laws were far less stringent than they later became and the pirating of such properties was the rule rather than the exception. In New York, London, and in other places there were wily schemers who did a lucrative business by stealing the texts of popular new plays, either by bribing some member of the cast or by planting copyists in the audiences who took down the dialogue, and peddling them to managers in the hinterlands.

One of the most celebrated of such instances was San Francisco's first production of *Pinafore,* which was put on at the Bush Street Theater on the afternoon of December 28, 1878, less than six months after that perennial favorite had had its world première in London. At the time, and for long thereafter, it was believed that this had been the first American production of the operetta. It was, however, a distinction it did not deserve, for later research revealed that Boston had beaten San Francisco by a little more than a month, having produced its own pirated version at the Boston Museum on the evening of November 25.

Those who saw this first local performance of *Pinafore* must have wondered what all the excitement was about. For, lacking stage directions, and with both dialogue and musical scores incomplete and garbled, the operetta proved anything but the rollicking comedy that was entrancing the Londoners. The San Francisco audiences appear to have been far more puzzled than entertained. Contributing to the general confusion was the fact that the male lead, dashing Ralph Rackstraw, who loved the Captain's daughter, was taken by Alice Oates, the company's leading lady—mainly, it was said, because she liked to dress up in male clothing. Moreover, in order to enliven the piece, the manager, Charles E. Locke, had supplemented Gilbert and Sullivan's songs with a number of others, all on nautical themes. Thus Alice Oates sang "The Death of Nelson" and "The Bay of Biscay O." Captain Corcoran rendered "Larboard Watch Ahoy," and the villain, Deadeye Dick, followed with "Rocked in the Cradle of the

Deep." Finally, Little Buttercup added still further to the confusion by dancing the "sailor's hornpipe."

One privileged to witness the performance later wrote: "The company did not suspect that the piece was a satire, literary, political, and musical; in fact, the performers had no idea what it was all about. Before they had finished, neither had the audience." The town's critics, naturally enough, had little good to say of this work that was reported to have convulsed the Londoners. "It might go in England," wrote one, "but it won't go here." His prophecy proved correct; after a single performance manager Locke withdrew it and in its place put on a melodrama, a type of entertainment better suited to the tastes of his audiences.

San Franciscans, however, had not seen the last of *Pinafore.* In the spring of the following year, a more complete and accurate version having become available, it was put on by a semiamateur group, with Emilie Melville playing Josephine. It had a run of several weeks. This convinced Locke that the piece after all had possibilities, and on June 9 it went on the boards again at the Bush Street, where it met with a much warmer reception. Thereafter, for well over two decades, *Pinafore* was one of the standbys both of touring troupes and local stock companies.

One of the places where it and numerous other musical shows were regularly put on was the Tivoli Opera House, known to several generations of music-loving San Franciscans as the Tiv. Founded in 1875 by "Pop" Kerling—who for the next thirty years nightly presided over its "upstairs" bar—it occupied a three-story frame building on Ellis Street a few doors from Market, a boxlike structure whose austere façade and prim picket fence gave it the appearance of a warehouse.

This, however, was grossly misleading, for inside was a

Bartlett Alley, Chinatown. Throughout the 1890s this was one of the centers of the town's booming red-light district.

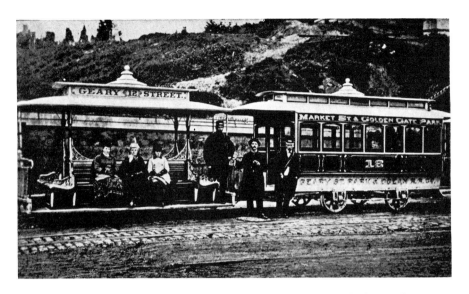

A Geary Street cable car. On fine days these open-air forward
units were popular with San Franciscans of all ages.

A Chinese opium den. This is typical of scores such in the Oriental
quarter in pre-fire days.

A Sunday afternoon on Sutro Heights. The public was welcomed to Adolph Sutro's elaborately landscaped gardens overlooking the Pacific.

The Terrace, Sutro Heights. Beyond are the Cliff House (the second of four to occupy the site) and Seal Rocks.

A Courtyard of the Midwinter Fair, 1894. One of its purposes was to publicize San Francisco's salubrious winter climate.

The Castle atop Telegraph Hill, 1899. The crowd is welcoming the return of a regiment of California Volunteers from the Philippines.

Lillie Hitchcock Coit, society belle and official mascot of
the town's volunteer firemen.

Duncan Nicol's Bank Exchange Saloon, Montgomery Block, long famous for its pisco punch, made with fiery Peruvian brandy.

One of Dr. Cogswell's drinking fountains, with a likeness of the donor (an ardent prohibitionist) proffering passers-by a glass of pure Spring Valley water.

Opposite: The end of "Lucky" Baldwin's hotel and theater. Until their destruction in the late 1890s these were favorite gathering places for San Franciscans on pleasure bent.

I NEVER SAW A PURPLE COW. I NEVER HOPE TO SEE ONE

BUT I CAN TELL YOU ANYHOW I'D RATHER SEE THAN BE ONE

The *Lark* presents *The Purple Cow*, the first appearance of Gelett Burgess's famous rhyme.

Nº I: 5 Cents

The Lark

' "Who'll be the Clerk?"
"I!" said the *Lark*.

The *Lark* makes its bow. The cover of Volume I, Number I of the town's precedent-breaking little periodical.

The Tivoli Opera House on Eddy Street, a favorite with music
lovers throughout the 1890s.

Ambrose Bierce, the most widely read—and feared—of the town's journalists.

Youthful Jack London, at the period when his Alaska stories were first bringing him renown.

Jack London's *The Snark* makes ready to sail. In the foreground,
left to right: James Hopper, Charmian London, George Sterling,
and Jack London.

Three literary lights at the Bohemian Club encampment on the Russian River; left to right: George Sterling, Stewart Edward White, Jack London.

Joaquin Miller at the Hights,
entertaining a group of admirers,
mostly feminine.

Frank Norris, one of the town's
prominent young writers during
the middle and late 1890s.

A life class at the California
School of Design, 1895.

William Keith in his studio, the
best known, and most prolific of
the town's artists.

The Hopkins mansion, Nob Hill. During the 1890s it housed the
city's leading art school.

The end of the Old Town—looking down Market Street on the morning of April 19, 1906.

combination beer garden and theater, with tables and greenery occupying the ground floor and, above, three balconies facing the stage. Between acts waiters circulated among the tables bearing trays of draught beer and, for those on the balconies, depositing the steins on little metal shelves which they attached to the backs of the seats ahead—all this for the convenience of those who preferred not to take their refreshment at one or another of the establishment's three bars.

What drew the crowds, however, was the quality of the entertainment. For over a period of more than a quarter century patrons could hear opera every night of the year, paying a modest fifty cents for the privilege. During eight of the twelve months light operas were presented—Gilbert and Sullivan being prime favorites throughout the 1880s and 1890s—and for the balance of the year the fare was grand opera. Moreover, San Franciscans stoutly maintained that the quality of the productions was unexcelled elsewhere in the country, regardless of the prices charged.

In the early 1890s, under the direction of William H. "Doc" Leahy, and with Paul Steindorff as orchestra leader, the Tiv reached its zenith. For Leahy, a hard taskmaster and shrewd judge of latent musical talent, combed the city and farther afield for promising beginners, putting them through a rigorous course of training, from which they emerged finished performers. One graduate of his chorus was Alice Nielsen; another was the soprano Luisa Tetrazzini, whom he discovered while on a trip to Mexico City, where the Italian company of which she was a minor member had become stranded. Leahy brought her back to San Francisco and cast her as Gilda in *Rigoletto*, in which role she scored a tremendous success with Tivoli audiences.

Years later, having risen to stardom, Tetrazzini returned to San Francisco in 1909 and, before an immense crowd, gave a Christmas Eve concert from a platform at the junction of Market, Geary, and Kearny streets. Two years later she gave a repeat performance at the same spot, drawing an even vaster throng and cementing for all time her position as the city's best-loved diva.

III.

San Francisco had other favorites besides the gracious Tetrazzini; from the beginning there was rarely a time when residents were not making folk heroes of someone, be it Lotta Crabtree or Mrs. Judah, early-day actresses, Thomas Starr King, eloquent preacher and orator during Civil War days, or any one of a dozen others.

During the 1890s it found a new popular idol, this time in the person of a handsome Irish lad named Jim Corbett. One of the numerous offspring of Patrick Corbett, who operated a livery stable on Hayes Street, young Jim grew up in the boisterous Hayes Valley district, briefly attended the St. Ignatius and Sacred Heart schools, and, having attained the ripe age of thirteen, went to work as messenger boy at the Nevada Bank, recently founded by Messrs. Mackay, Fair, Flood, and O'Brien, owners of immensely rich silver mines at Virginia City.

The personable youth remained at the bank for six years, rising to the post of assistant paying teller. However, it presently grew clear that his interests—and talents—lay in other directions. For from his earliest school days he had been uncommonly handy with his fists, and in his father's stable and on the neighboring sandhills had frequently demonstrated his prowess, usually at the expense of boys older and bigger than himself. Soon after he went to work at the bank he joined the Olympic Club and, under the tutorship of the club's boxing instructor, quickly picked up the rudiments of the fistic art.

Corbett's first important fight was with another local youth who was also to make a name for himself in the annals of professional pugilism, a lad named Joe Choynski. Their pitched battle—a bare-knuckle slug fest in the hills near the ocean—came about because of the boasting of two elder brothers of the pair, who worked side by side at the auditor's office at the City Hall, each of whom had been bragging about the boxing skill of his kid brother.

From their first encounter Corbett emerged victor, and soon thereafter joined the ranks of the professionals, appearing frequently in four-round matches, most of which he won, and slowly gaining both experience and a considerable local following. Then, in 1890, he was, by a happy accident, suddenly projected into national prominence. This came about in the following manner: A weekly paper had recently been launched in San Francisco, the *California Illustrated World*, and the first number bore on its cover a picture of Corbett in his fighting togs, the caption reading: "The Coming Champion of the World!" Somehow a copy found its way to New Orleans, near which city John L. Sullivan and Jake Kilrain had recently fought for the title, Sullivan emerging victor after a struggle that lasted seventy-five rounds.

Kilrain, a great favorite with New Orleans fans, was then angling for a return match, and on the lookout for an opponent for a six-round bout to be held there during Mardi Gras. Those whose names were suggested were all turned down by Kilrain, who had no wish to meet an experienced fighter at that stage of his comeback campaign. Finally, someone produced a copy of the California weekly proclaiming Corbett —who was completely unknown outside San Francisco—as the coming world's champion. Promptly a telegram was dispatched West challenging him to box Kilrain for a purse of $2,500, the winner to take $2,000, the loser $500.

Despite grave misgivings on the part of his friends, Corbett wired his acceptance and set off for the scene of the carnage. While en route, during a stop at a way station in New Mexico, Corbett was sprinting up and down the station platform when a westbound train pulled in. Among its passengers was John W. Mackay, president of the Nevada Bank. Mackay recognized his former paying teller and demanded to know what he was doing there. When the youth announced proudly that he was on his way to New Orleans to fight the great Kilrain, Mackay replied gruffly: "I hope he gives you a damn good licking!"

As it turned out, that hope was not realized. Although the New Orleans sports were offering 4 to 1 on Kilrain and even money that the challenger—who weighed 165 pounds to the other's 210—would not last three rounds, when the pair got into the ring Corbett's superior boxing skill at once became evident. For six rounds he punched the veteran at will, easily avoiding the other's roundhouse swings, and at the end the referee awarded him the decision.

His unexpected defeat of Kilrain not only made young Corbett the idol of San Francisco's sporting fraternity, but put him in line for a shot at Sullivan's championship crown. A long step in that direction was his fight, on May 21, 1891, with Peter Jackson, a clever Negro boxer who had met and defeated every leading heavyweight in Australia, England, and the United States, excepting Sullivan, who refused to meet one of his race. The Corbett-Jackson bout, put on in San Francisco by the California Athletic Club for a purse of $10,000—the largest ever offered up to that time—went sixty-one rounds, at the end of which time, both men having reached the point of complete exhaustion, the match was declared a draw and the purse divided 50–50 between them.

With his winnings—which, it developed, was not the promised $5,000 but only half that sum—Corbett set up one of his brothers in a bar and café at the corner of Battery and Bush streets. With its big sign, "Corbett's," over the door, the place became a favorite rendezvous of the town's sports and remained so until it was destroyed in the 1906 fire.

Following the Jackson bout, a match with the great John L. became Corbett's consuming ambition. The other, however, was barnstorming about the country in a play called *Honest Hearts and Willing Hands,* and in no hurry to defend his championship; it was, hence, not until the summer of 1892 that a meeting was arranged. It took place in New Orleans on September 7 of that year, and again the challenger was on the short end of 4 to 1 odds. The fight, a vicious one from the offset, went the first few rounds without either gaining any marked advantage. As it progressed, however, Corbett's superior boxing skill began to tell. Sullivan's bull-like rushes at his agile opponent, plus the punishment he had taken from the other's left jabs, gradually weakened him, and in the twenty-first round a series of rights and lefts to the jaw sent him crashing to the floor for a count of ten. Corbett, at twenty-six, was the world's champion.

He held the title five years, meantime meeting Charley Mitchell, Tom Sharkey, and several others, then signing for a meeting with a promising newcomer named "Ruby Bob" Fitzsimmons. The Corbett-Fitzsimmons bout had an involved history, for opposition to prize fighting in general, and to championship contests in particular, had by then grown strong among churchmen and others all over the country. The result was that whenever a site was chosen pressure was brought to bear on state and local authorities to forbid it.

The fight originally was scheduled at Dallas, Texas; the promoters began erecting a big outdoor arena there and the boxers took up training quarters nearby. Thereupon the Texas governor announced that the affair would not be permitted within the borders of that state. A new location was accordingly chosen, this time at Hot Springs, Arkansas, and again preparations were far advanced when the governor—who, it was claimed, had given advance assurances that he would not interfere—forbade the match.

Once more fighters, promoters, and camp followers were forced to move on, this time to Carson City, Nevada, where the much-postponed battle finally took place on March 17, 1897. On this occasion, however, Corbett faced a man who was as crafty a ring strategist as was he himself. Before a crowd of 20,000—the largest, up to that time, that had ever witnessed a fight—the two battled on fairly even grounds until the fourteenth round, when "Ruby Bob's" celebrated solar plexus blow found its mark and Corbett went down for the count.

After his loss of the championship Corbett's one aim was to regain it. Fitzsimmons, however, refused to meet him again, taking on instead a young fighter named James J. Jeffries—who had been one of Corbett's sparring partners at Carson City—and losing the title to him at Coney Island on June 9, 1899. Some eleven months later Corbett and Jeffries met at the same spot, Jeffries winning by a knockout in the twenty-third round. A full three years later, at San Francisco on August 14, 1903, the pair were rematched, Jeffries this time stopping the fading ex-champion in the tenth, whereupon Gentleman Jim hung up his gloves for good.

However, following his retirement from the ring he by no means lapsed into obscurity. Always an actor at heart, he made numerous stage appearances during the next decade, and although he was then living in the East, he frequently returned to San Francisco, where his every appearance, whether in a play, a vaudeville sketch, or on the lecture platform, was a signal for a gathering of the clans. San Francisco rarely forgot those who had once been its idols.

CHAPTER 6

Journalism Rampant

I.

Before the completion of the Central Pacific Railroad in 1869 ended California's isolation from the rest of the nation, its residents were for the most part obliged to provide their own means of entertainment and recreation. One result was that throughout the 1850s and 1860s there sprang up in San Francisco a profusion of weekly journals catering to the interests of literary-minded citizens, and in the columns of which appeared the first work of a group of writers who later became well known.

By the time the 1890s rolled around many of these periodicals had fallen by the wayside; others, however, were still being published and read. The oldest was the *News-Letter*, still under the editorship of its founder, an Englishman named Frederick Marriott, who had earlier been with the *London Illustrated News*. In 1868 the *News-Letter*, which specialized in satire, introduced a newcomer named Ambrose Bierce to local readers; some years earlier it had run a series of burlesques by another promising tyro, F. Bret Harte.

One of the *News-Letter's* chief rivals in the beginning 1890s was the *Wasp*. Established in 1870 by two German immigrants, the Korbel brothers, it was from its founding given over to exposure of local shams and corruption, which it treated with a stinging candor that fully lived up to its name. The *Wasp's* chief claim to fame, however, is the fact that it was the first American magazine to introduce a feature that was soon to become popular all over the country; namely, colored cartoons. For years its two middle pages were each week given over to such drawings, executed by a group of highly competent artists and treating ironically of subjects—political or social—currently in the public eye.

In its text the *Wasp's* treatment of such matters was no less entertaining. Thus in its issue of July 22, 1893, appeared the following:

Our esteemed contemporary, "The Examiner," asks anent the youth who shot his playmate in Los Angeles: "Why should a boy of fourteen be allowed to carry a revolver?" That's right. There is no sense to it. There are hardly enough revolvers to go around for the married men who want to make themselves widowers, the jealous lovers who keep Coroner Hughes busy, and all the adult celebrities who need firearms to keep the newspapers readable. It is a blame shame to let small boys waste good pistols and powder in these lively times.

A third member of this group of weeklies was the *Argonaut*. This journal was launched in 1877 and, under the editorship successively of Frank Pixley, Fred Somers, and Jerome Hart, was ever receptive to new writers. In politics it consistently reflected the viewpoint of the Southern Pacific Railroad, thereby bringing it into frequent—and usually violent—conflict with other local papers, most of which were avowed enemies of that corporation.

It was, however, in its literary columns that the *Argonaut*

achieved its widest renown. A list of its contributors constitutes a roll call of talented local authors throughout the period. These include Bierce—whose column, "The Prattler,"
began with its first number—Gertrude Atherton, Geraldine
Bonner, Ina Coolbrith, Emma Frances Dawson, W. C. Morrow, Richard Realf, Charles H. Shinn, Charles Warren Stoddard, Sam Davis, Frank Norris, Jack London, Will and
Wallace Irwin, and a host of others.

Another weekly that flourished briefly in the 1890s, and
had an uncommonly large audience during the few months
it was published, was *Arthur McEwen's Letter*. Its founder,
born in Scotland and taken to Canada as a child, had reached
California in the early 1870s, a youth of nineteen, and for the
next dozen years had worked on a succession of papers in
San Francisco and the towns of the interior. A fluent writer,
with a pretty talent for invective—a quality then highly regarded by western newspaper readers—he was serving as
editor of the local *Post* when young Hearst, having recently
taken over the *Examiner*, lured him away and installed him
as editorial writer on his rejuvenated journal.

McEwen continued to hold that post for six years, during
which time he made the paper's editorial page the liveliest in
town, his comments on issues and persons in the public eye
setting new standards of frankness even in that era of uninhibited journalism. It was he who once stated the *Examiner's*
aim in words that for years after were quoted as a neat sum-
ming up of the Hearst newspaper creed. Any issue, wrote he,
the front page of which failed to elicit a "Gee whiz!" from its
readers was a failure, whereas the second page ought to bring
forth a "Holy Moses!" and the third an astounded "God
Almighty!"

Sometime in 1893 McEwen left the *Examiner* and launched
a weekly potpourri of news and comment called "Arthur

McEwen's Letter," which appeared in a number of papers up and down the coast. One of his "Letters" was given over to a vitriolic attack on M. H. de Young, owner of the *Chronicle*. The public's response to that onslaught was so enthusiastic that McEwen was encouraged to try his hand at lambasting other local dignitaries who seemed to him to merit the same treatment. He accordingly abandoned his syndicated column and began the publication of a weekly paper bearing the same title; that is, *Arthur McEwen's Letter*. Its first number appeared on February 17, 1894, a modest four-page sheet that in its chaste typography suggested, in the words of one reader, that it might be devoted to "an account of the proceedings of the bishops' convention or the annual report of an eleemosynary institution."

A reading of its columns, however, quickly dispelled that impression. Virtually the entire first issue was given over to a scathing attack on the *Chronicle* owner, in which that individual was held up to ridicule on the score of his egoism, political and social ambitions, business ethics, and much else. This was the sort of literary fare readers of the day found exactly to their liking and the presses were kept busy day and night to meet the demand, the total run exceeding 15,000. Spurred on by that initial success, the editor followed the same pattern in succeeding numbers, not only continuing his lampooning of De Young but launching similar attacks on other well-known figures, Collis Huntington, the Crockers, Tevises, Fairs, political boss Chris Buckley, and a variety of others.

In his treatment of none of these, however, was he able to muster quite the same entertaining blend of irony and ridicule that had distinguished his onslaughts on Mike de Young. The consequence was that after the first few issues circulation began to fall off. Disregarding the advice of friends that he resume his attacks on the *Chronicle's* owner—and thus, as he commented wryly, convert his paper into the *Weekly Mike* —he continued publication some weeks longer before, on June 15, 1895, throwing in the sponge.

One of McEwen's partners in that short-lived enterprise was a young lawyer with political ambitions named Franklin K. Lane, who was later to become Secretary of the Interior under President Wilson. McEwen himself presently rejoined the Hearst organization as editorial writer, both in San Francisco and New York, and subsequently held a number of important journalistic posts. He died in 1907.

Still another weekly that, entering the already crowded field, yet made a lasting name for itself was the *Wave*. Beginning in 1888 as a society sheet designed to attract patronage to the Southern Pacific's big resort hotel, Del Monte, on the Monterey peninsula, it was presently moved to San Francisco, where its editor, John O'Hara Cosgrove, gathered about him a group of bright young contributors. The prize of the lot was, of course, Frank Norris, who joined the staff in the mid-1890s and, until he left for the East several years later, contributed a steady stream of material—short stories, articles, interviews, and parodies—to its columns.

It was then the custom for all the weeklies, including those that normally were entirely staff-written, to bring out special issues several times each year: spring and summer numbers, and at Christmas and Thanksgiving. To these, outside contributions—drawings, fiction, poems, and factual articles— were solicited. These "Special Numbers," which sometimes had a bulk of a hundred pages or more, were an important outlet for the town's numerous artists and scribblers.

Besides the weeklies, and the long-established *Overland Monthly,* the free-lance writers and artists of the day had yet another outlet for their wares. Several of the local newspapers, notably the *Call,* the *Chronicle,* and the *Examiner,* issued Sunday magazine sections, which were mainly given over to stories, verse, and articles by local writers, the day of wide-spread syndication of such material being still in the future. Thus with a variety of markets for his productions close at hand, it is not surprising that the San Francisco of the day offered a fertile field to the beginning scribe, and that more writers of note served their apprenticeship on the local journals during the 1890s than at any other period of the city's history.

II.

Among newspapers, the *Examiner* had by the beginning of the 1890s shouldered its way close to the top. The story of its rise is an engaging one. Founded in the mid-1860s, it had in the fall of 1880 passed to George Hearst, wealthy mine owner, who used it as a means of furthering his political ambitions. On his election, seven years later, to the United States Senate, he was prevailed upon to turn over the property to his twenty-four-year-old son.

That transfer of ownership aroused no particular comment at the time, for the little six-page sheet was one of the less important journals in the crowded, highly competitive field. It had not been long under the direction of its new owner, however, before there was a widespread raising of eyebrows. For it soon became clear that the new owner had certain fixed ideas—most of them highly unorthodox—as to how an up-and-coming newspaper ought to be run. Moreover, being plentifully supplied with cash, he lost no time in putting these into effect.

One of his first moves was to order new presses and other

mechanical equipment and to increase the paper's size from six to eight pages on weekdays and from twelve to sixteen on Sundays. Moreover, he set about raiding the editorial rooms of the other journals, luring away many of their ablest men and assembling a staff that far outshone those of its rivals. Among those hired during the first few months were T. T. Williams, who was installed as city editor, Ed Hamilton, political reporter, Arthur McEwen, and, as columnist, the widely admired—and even more widely feared—Ambrose Bierce.

Years later Bierce recalled his first meeting with the man for whom he was to work, off and on, for the next twenty years. The journalist, who was then out of a job—his column, "The Prattler," in the *Argonaut* having been discontinued some months earlier—one day heard a gentle knock on the door of his Oakland lodgings. On answering he found what he described as "a young man, the youngest man, it seemed to me, that I had ever confronted," standing on the steps.

Bierce did not invite his caller inside. Instead, he merely said: "Well," and waited.

" 'I am from the San Francisco *Examiner*,' he explained in a voice like the fragrance of violets made audible, and backed a little away.

" 'Oh,' I said, 'you come from Mr. Hearst?'

"Then that unearthly child lifted his blue eyes and cooed: 'I *am* Mr. Hearst.' "

Bierce's first column appeared on March 27, 1887, less than a month after Hearst assumed command. Thereafter for nine years, until his boss transferred him to Washington, D.C., his "Prattle" appeared each Sunday on the editorial page, his amusing and usually vitriolic comments on the passing show becoming required reading for thousands all over the northern half of the state.

The rejuvenated paper had, however, a plenitude of other features. Among young Hearst's ten-strikes was a girl reporter, Winifred Sweet, who joined up in 1889 and remained a fixture on the staff even longer than Bierce. Because she was, as the paper once boasted, "intelligent, brave, industrious, self-possessed, and bothered with no silly-girl prejudices as to what a lady should or should not do in a profession," she was given a series of picturesque assignments that alternately shocked and entertained the town.

One of the first of these was to interview a number of local "divorce lawyers" and, posing as a discontented wife, learn how easy it was to shunt off an unwanted mate. "It's a common thing," she wrote, "for a woman to apply for a divorce during her husband's absence, on any grounds she may see fit. When he returns he finds himself divorced on some vile charge which has, perhaps, not the slightest foundation."

Another of her stories—all of which appeared under her pen name, "Annie Laurie"—had to do with exposing the treatment the public received at the local emergency hospital. Dressed in shabby clothes and feigning illness, she sank down on a Market Street sidewalk during the busiest part of an afternoon and awaited developments. A crowd gathered and after some delay she was hustled into a police van and jolted over the cobbles to the hospital. On arriving there, so she reported, "one by one every person present stopped near me and sniffed my breath. The policeman was the last of all. 'No, I can't smell any whisky,' said he. 'I wish to heaven I could say as much for you,' thought I . . ." She was given an emetic of hot water and mustard and turned loose—to return to the *Examiner* office and write a scathing story on the brutality and general incompetence of the physician in charge.

The result was that the latter, having been suspended by

the Board of Health appeared at the office of the paper, his manner indicating that, in the words of that journal, he was "spoiling for a fight." There he was met, "not by a sick female patient," but by the burly city editor. After he had "received a couple of punches," the story concludes, "he lay on his back whining like a whipped cur." Clearly the *Examiner* of that period had no leanings toward the pusillanimous type of journalism.

All through the 1890s the indomitable Annie kept the paper's readers entertained by similar exploits. She became successively a Salvation Army lass; got a job in a local fruit cannery (where she received twenty-six cents for eight hours of backbreaking work); exposed the venders of quack cosmetics who foisted "valueless and poisonous drugs" at high prices on the trusting females of the town; sampled the food served at the training table of the Stanford football team; interviewed the madam of one of the town's leading bawdyhouses, and much else.

Meantime other reporters were performing feats no less spectacular. "All the leading sensations are graphically reported," stated one of the paper's early advertisements, and throughout the next decade that policy was faithfully adhered to. In 1889 a staff member named Frank Peltret was assigned to have himself committed to the state insane asylum at Stockton and learn at first hand how inmates were treated there. Peltret boarded a steamer for the valley town, jumped overboard while en route, and, on being fished out of the river, explained that it had been his intention to visit his sister, "who lived in the beautiful water." This seemed evidence enough that he was crazy; he was accordingly committed to the asylum, kept there a month, and on his release wrote a graphic account of his experiences.

Three months later—this time to test the efficiency of the

lifesaving apparatus on board the transbay ferries—another reporter, "accompanied by two artists, a time-keeper . . . and a sinking sensation in the pit of his stomach," went aboard the ferryboat *Oakland* and when it had reached mid-bay managed to fall over its rail. After a brief but exciting struggle with the undertow in the wake of the vessel, the victim paddled about, closely observing efforts to rescue him. His first discovery was that the life buoy that had been tossed in after him was of little use, since it lay low in the water and could not readily be seen. "Each buoy," he commented later, "should carry a little stick with a flag on it."

The ferry stopped and the crew had one of its small boats in the water in a matter of three minutes and forty seconds after the cry of "Man overboard" had been sounded—this the victim considered about par for the course. On being deposited once more on the ferry's deck, "hatless, coatless, boot-less, cold and clammy," he heard one onlooker remark sternly, "I guess he won't get drunk again in a hurry"—at which point "about a dozen men rushed at him with glasses of whisky." Being thoroughly chilled, he took a few sips, which elicited the comment that "ferryboat whisky is pretty hot tipple," then hurried down to the boiler room to dry off. His story, which was featured the following Sunday, that of September 2, 1888, stated, sensibly enough, that "The general public is recommended not to fall overboard too often."

Stunts of that sort kept the town amused all through the early 1890s. In April 1891 a reporter was assigned to put on old clothes and try his luck as a street beggar. At the end of a full day he thus listed the result: "Receipts, $1.95, plus an orange; expenses, 15¢; profit, $1.80, and the orange." In conclusion he stated: "Being 'broke' no longer has any horrors for me. With a plausible story, a sanctimonious exterior, a fair proportion of hypocrisy and the exercise of a little judg-

ment any man can make a living by begging in San Francisco
. . . provided one's tastes are not too aristocratic."

Yet another exploit—this one early in 1892—that aroused
widespread interest among *Examiner* readers, was that of
Robert Duncan Milne, a well-known writer of pseudo-scientific fiction, who took the Keeley Cure for alcoholism. His
full-page report, which appeared on Sunday, January 17,
described the treatment in detail and highly praised its effec-
tiveness. In Milne's case, however, the cure could hardly have
been permanent, for less than a month later an *Examiner*
editorial commented that "the lapse of Mr. Milne within two
weeks after his discharge as cured . . . will be taken by many
as justifying the sneers and scoffing of the regular physicians
against Dr. Keeley's methods. This view of the case, though
natural, does injustice to the treatment."

The editorial went on to state that Milne "took the bichlo-
ride treatment merely as an experiment prompted by an enlightened curiosity. No desire for sobriety prompted him to
seek relief from alcoholic craving . . ." In an adjoining column appeared a letter from Dr. G. E. Gussdorff, manager of
the local Keeley Institute, stating: "He [Milne] seems to us
to have had no wish to be cured . . . thinking that all the
pleasure he had had in life was gotten while under the influence of liquor and believing that he could have more pleasure in the future drunk than sober. If we are correct in our
judgment, Mr. Milne will go back to drinking just because,
according to his ideas, a state of drunkenness is preferable to
a state of sobriety . . ."

One can readily understand why the *Examiner* was avidly
read over the town's breakfast tables throughout the 1890s.

III.

Nor was the paper's rapid rise in public favor—circulation figures jumped from 18,000 to 57,000 during the first year under the new management—unregarded by the competing journals. A fierce rivalry promptly developed, and for a time the editorial brickbats flew thick and fast. Many of the *Examiner's* thrusts at its contemporaries were couched in terms of none too gentle irony, as when it congratulated the *Morning Call* on its enterprise in "publishing in small installments the story *Allan Quartermain*, by H. Rider Haggard." Having pointed out that "the novel has already been published complete in four installments in the 'Examiner,' and cheap editions have been on sale in every city news-stand since our last installment appeared," it went on to state magnanimously: "But the 'Call' should not be discouraged by this circumstance. Its intention was excellent, and we trust its future efforts to furnish literature to its readers will continue . . ."

In similar vein it, a few days later, cast an eye over the sartorial splendors—and shortcomings—of the town's editors. Loring Pickering, joint proprietor of the *Bulletin,* came off well, the critic commenting that "his decorous black broadcloth is ever well-brushed, his boots polished, his linen clean and his plug hat within a year or two of the latest thing." Mr. Pickering's partner, however, George K. Fitch, was more severely dealt with. "He is undoubtedly within his rights," the *Examiner* stated, "in growling through the *Bulletin* at everybody that likes the city of today better than the town as it was in '55, but he assuredly is not justified in walking abroad before dark." The co-owner of the *Examiner's* arch rival, the *Chronicle,* was dismissed in a few words, thus: "Mr. de

Young is frequently seen in clothing fit for a gentleman."
The writer's choicest satire, however, was reserved for
Colonel John P. Irish, a popular orator of the day, then editor
of the *Call*, which was one of the few papers friendly to the
Southern Pacific Railroad. Among Irish's many eccentricities
was his refusal to wear a collar or necktie. Of him the reporter
wrote:

"Colonel Irish—well, professional courtesy restrains remark. His speeches at country fairs are lovely, and he can
garland a new sewer proposition with the greenery of his
rhetoric till the listener wants to live in a drain. But after all
the Colonel could do more for his adopted state by the simple
act of buying a collar and putting it on than all his noble
oratory can accomplish. It is surprising that the railroads,
intent as they are upon increasing their passenger traffic, do
not insist upon the Colonel wearing a collar openly and
proudly . . ."

Throughout the decade the *Examiner* and the *Chronicle*
carried on a bitter feud over which had the largest circulation,
each accusing the other of all manner of nefarious schemes in
order to appear the leader. In November of 1895 the *Chronicle*, in substantiation of its charge that its rival was daily
printing far more papers than the public bought, published
photographs of a heavily loaded dray purportedly carrying
off copies of unsold *Examiners* to a wastepaper dealer. Next
day the *Examiner* commented: "It will be observed that between the time of the loading and the start for Sutton &
Partridge's establishment the horse on the left turned black
and his mate turned white. Doubtless they were frightened at
being photographed 'Especially for the *Chronicle.*' "

In the same issue appeared an editorial—headed "Put Up
or Shut Up"—accusing the *Chronicle* of "forging pictures
of a wagon and inventing loads of papers that never existed,"

and offering to bet its rival's owners $5,000 that "the 'Examiner's' circulation affidavit is correct, and $5,000 more that the 'Chronicle's' statement claiming 68,000 circulation is false . . ." Next day the *Chronicle* retorted by accusing its rival of having falsified its circulation figures with a "cooked-up set of books, prepared with the evident design of bunkoing," and adding that it "refused to be fooled into entering into an arrangement in which, like a card sharp, its adversary has all the advantages which result from the employment of what is known as 'a cold deck,' a term with which we infer our contemporary must be very familiar, judging from its readiness to resort to the methods of a gambler to settle disputes."

The controversy raged for weeks, during which the sales of both papers rose sharply as an interested public followed the daily exchanges and wondered what was coming next. In the heat of battle personalities were by no means excluded, the *Examiner* on November 6 running this item:

"M. H. de Young, the proprietor of the 'Chronicle,' arrived home yesterday . . . It has been widely reported that Mr. de Young would come back a changed man. Rumors were rife that he had bought himself one of those rippling, wavy French Toupees that look as though they grow right on a man's head. He introduced the toupee at the Waldorf dinner in New York last week, when Chauncey Depew congratulated him upon looking like one of the Sutherland Sisters with her hair cut short. It was hoped that he would display the toupee to Californians after he crossed the state line. But Mr. de Young is a modest man. He did not want to paralyze people with a renaissance." Accompanying the story was a three-column caricature—drawn by a young staff artist named Jimmy Swinnerton—showing De Young's normally bald head crowned by flowing locks, and bearing the caption: "False on the face of it!"

Clearly San Franciscans of the period opened their morning papers prepared for anything—and were seldom disappointed.

IV.

Toward the close of 1892, some five years after the new owner had assumed charge, the *Examiner* scored one of the most sensational feats of its by no means humdrum career. That was the publication, on October 7, of what purported to be a firsthand interview with a pair of train robbers for whom scores of law officers had been hunting for the better part of four years. The names of these latter-day Robin Hoods were Chris Evans and John Sontag.

At the time—in the late 1880s—when this pair began to operate, the Concord coaches of the pioneers had, in all save the remoter corners of the state, been displaced by the iron horse. Moreover, by then the widely held belief that the coming of the railroads would usher in a period of prosperity for all had been severely shaken. This was particularly true in the San Joaquin Valley, where, in 1880, a long-standing feud between the Southern Pacific and a group of farmers had flared into open warfare during which seven men were killed.

This "Battle of Mussel Slough" opened up a breach between the railroad and residents of the valley that a full generation failed to cure. Hard times in the region during the 1880s and early 1890s added to the ill-feeling, the hard-pressed ranchers and merchants attributing their troubles to high freight rates, subsidies to favored shippers, and other tactics employed by the corporation. It was on this situation that, some years later, Frank Norris based his novel, *The Octopus*. It was, too, because of the bitter anti-railroad feeling throughout the valley that when the company's trains began to be boarded by a pair of masked men, who overpowered the engine crews, dynamited the express cars, and made off with whatever valuables they contained, the prevailing sentiment was firmly on the side of the unknown enterprisers.

The general opinion was that they were local men, who, like their neighbors, had suffered wrongs at the hands of the railroad and had taken that means of settling old scores. Thus from the beginning conditions were favorable for the creating of a pair of folk heroes, worthy successors to the romantic road agents of an earlier day.

Between February 22, 1889, and September 2, 1891, the bandits staged three train robberies, during which three men were killed. Each time they, themselves, escaped scot-free. On the fourth attempt, however, they left behind clues that clearly established their identity.

Nonetheless, the pair managed to elude the posses that were presently scouring the countryside and made their way by unfrequented trails into the Sierra fastnesses to the east, a region with which they were both familiar, having spent several summers locating and working mining claims there.

Then began a grim game of hide-and-seek that lasted for the better part of two years, and meanwhile held the unflagging interest of thousands all over the West. By that time rewards for the pair's capture had reached the impressive figure of $10,000, a sum that drew not only the regular law enforcement officers but scores of amateur manhunters into the area. The pair, aided by their knowledge of the country, and with the help of residents of the little mountain communities —who resented this influx of hordes of strangers from the lowlands—successfully eluded capture, meantime living in reasonable comfort at their secret hideaways.

During that period, however, they had another brush with

the law. Some six weeks after their flight to the mountains and having, as Evans later reported, grown tired of their own cooking, they left their hiding place and made their way to the cabin of an acquaintance named Jim Young on nearby Pine Ridge. Unknown to them, those directing the hunt had stationed a man to watch the cabin, and the lookout, having seen Evans and Sontag enter, slipped away and gave the alarm.

The result was that while their meal was being prepared the pair observed a posse ride up and stop before the gate. Two of the group dismounted and started toward the cabin. When they had approached to within twenty feet of the door, the bandits thrust the muzzles of their sawed-off shotguns through the windows and pulled the triggers. As their victims fell, the two dashed out the door, meantime firing into the group at the gate. These, taken by surprise, broke ranks and scattered in confusion. Then, at the moment the last of the posse had fled and the battle seemed over, the shooting flared up again. Andy McGinnis, one of the two who had fallen within the yard, had brought his rifle into play, a ball striking Sontag in the arm and inflicting a flesh wound. Before the officer could reload, Evans's gun silenced him. That was the end of the carnage; the pair made their way back to their hideaway, leaving behind the bodies of two officers.

The encounter on Pine Ridge further intensified the already high public interest in the manhunt, and from then on all San Francisco newspapers had reporters permanently assigned to the story. These, stationing themselves in the sheriffs' offices at Fresno or Visalia, or trailing along with the posses in the mountains, forwarded daily dispatches that were prominently displayed on the front pages of their journals. It was then, as the winter of 1892–93 was about to close down and bring a temporary halt to the manhunt, that the *Examiner* scored its sensational beat: no less than an interview with the pair for whom hundreds of men had been vainly hunting for months.

V.

The story—it appeared on the morning of October 7, 1892 —was promptly branded a hoax, not only by the *Examiner's* competitors but by the law enforcement officials. But a close reading of the dispatch, which was written by the debonair "Petey" Bigelow, one of the paper's star reporters, carried conviction, for his narrative was so straightforward, and fortified with such a wealth of detail—including columns of direct quotations from the bandits themselves giving their versions of the events of recent weeks—that little by little even the doubters grew convinced that Bigelow had in fact visited the pair and got their stories at first hand.

The precise means by which he was able to accomplish that feat has long been a matter of debate. One version is that when he left San Francisco he carried in an inner pocket of his stylish, London-made jacket $500 of *Examiner* money in crisp $100 bills; that he went directly to the Evans cottage at Visalia, made himself and his errand known to the bandit's wife, and offered to turn the bills over to her if she could arrange an interview.

That, however, was too prosaic a yarn to find many adherents. The most widely accepted version was far more picturesque. By it, the dapper little journalist had slipped unobtrusively into the valley town and had spent his days lounging about its bars and hotel lobbies, confiding to all who would listen his wish to interview the hunted men and present to the world their side of their feud with the greedy railroad corporation. This, so the story goes, continued for weeks, while Petey's fine raiment grew steadily more bedraggled and his once neatly trimmed beard became matted and unkempt, but still nothing happened. Then at last came the hoped-for break. One day a stranger slipped into a chair beside him in a hotel lobby, heard his by then familiar story, and at its end told him to be on hand at a certain hour the following night at a designated spot on the edge of town, and to come prepared for a long, hard trip.

Whatever version is the true one is immaterial; the important point is that Petey did in fact join the bandits at their mountain retreat. His first *Examiner* story was followed the next day by a second, in which he gave some details of his arduous journey into the hills. Some—but by no means all. For, as he pointed out, he had given his word that he would divulge no information as to the outlaws' whereabouts that would be useful to their pursuers. But he made it clear that the spot was cunningly concealed and that to reach it from the valley involved a long and difficult climb. His description of the region traversed was a model of calculated vagueness. "I set out," wrote he, "for the vicinity of the Kings River. This is a broad territory and seemed to me to consist chiefly of mountains about 6,000 or 7,000 feet high."

Although he did not state how many companions he had on the journey, his story makes it clear that a considerable caravan made its way to what he termed "the lair of the bandits." He had been permitted to join a party of friends bearing supplies for the pair. "The last of their winter stock of provisions," stated he, "was being got in on the backs of tiny burros." The meeting place he described as "a small house stationed in a tiny gulch that overlooks the great Fresno plain." There, admitting to "a pronounced inclination toward excitement," he joined the hunted pair, sat down with them on the edge of their bed, and during the next several hours filled page after page of his notebook with the answers given his questions.

Only one untoward incident marred that historic interview. The reporter presently unbuttoned his coat, thereby revealing, pinned to his shirt, his nickel-plated press badge. At sight of it the friendly atmosphere that had prevailed abruptly vanished. "Sontag scowled," wrote Bigelow, "and said something about 'detective.'" The other hastened to explain the true nature of the emblem and gradually the tension eased. "Yet," he added, "I believe they were still somewhat doubtful as to its meaning." The interview proceeded, the pair stoutly denying they had had any hand in the train robberies, picturing themselves as victims of the ruthlessness of the railroad's minions, and contending that, given an opportunity, they could prove themselves innocent of any wrongdoing.

Petey's interview of course made a tremendous stir, and the *Examiner* was not slow to congratulate itself on the journalistic enterprise that had brought it about. "What the sheriffs and their posses and innumerable detectives, stimulated by great money rewards and animated by a desire for vengeance, have so far utterly failed to do, an 'Examiner' reporter has done," it triumphantly stated in an editorial on October 8. The same issue contained a column-long story tracing the career of the reporter and listing other difficult assignments he had carried out while a member of the staff.

Ten days later the paper, stung by continuing jibes of rival editors hinting that the much-advertised Bigelow interview was a fake, again came to Petey's defense. Replying to a letter from a reader, it stated on October 18:

"Of course the 'Examiner' will vouch for the genuineness of the interview . . . Sundry contemporaries affect disbelief . . . That is to be expected. It is much easier and cheaper for a lethargic, back-number newspaper to sneer at the enterprise of a modern, wide-awake journal's enterprise in getting the news than it is to rival it. The 'Examiner' spends more money for news right along than all the rest of the San Francisco press put together, and it is so fortunate as to be able to command the brains necessary to make its large expenditure effective and profitable . . ."

The rest of the Evans-Sontag saga can be briefly told. Early in June 1893, some eight months after the Bigelow interview, the pair made their way down from the mountains, bent on paying a visit to the Evans family at their Visalia cottage. Somehow word of their plan reached the ears of the law, and groups of officers were stationed at several points along the route they were expected to follow. That strategy paid off. On the morning of June 12 four deputy sheriffs, waiting at a spot in the foothills called Stone Corral, spotted the pair as they approached, their intention being to hide their rifles in a nearby straw pile before continuing on to town.

Since the pair were expert marksmen, no attempt was made to capture them alive; instead, from their points of concealment, the deputies opened fire. Both men were struck by that first salvo; Evans eventually recovered but Sontag received a wound from which he died several weeks later. Nonetheless, they brought their own weapons into play and the shooting continued until Evans, making a break for freedom, was struck again. Badly wounded, he yet made a temporary getaway, only to be picked up later that day at a nearby farmhouse. Both men were lodged in the Fresno County jail, where Sontag presently died and his partner, having recovered, was held for trial.

But the drama was still far from over. In order to raise funds for the survivor's defense, a play—written by two local newspapermen—was put on the boards at San Francisco. Titled *Evans and Sontag; or, the Visalia Bandits*, the six-act melodrama purported to tell the story of the pair's wrongs at the hands of the railroad, and its star—a stroke of pure genius, this—was Evans's comely sixteen-year-old daughter Eva.

The show opened on September 19, 1893, and in his review the next morning the *Examiner's* critic stated that while it definitely belonged to the "blank cartridge school of drama," the capacity audience had greeted it with tremendous applause. Eva Evans was easily the favorite of the spectators, and a busy evening she had of it: spurning the advances of the villain—who, of course, was a railroad detective—barring the cottage door with her shapely arm to permit her father and lover—Sontag—to escape, and, disguised in frayed but becoming boy's clothes, hurrying into the mountains to warn the fugitives of danger. "When it is remembered that she is only sixteen," concluded the *Examiner's* tribute, "and that up to a week or so ago she was totally ignorant of anything connected with the stage, her work was really surprising." The show had a considerable run at the National Theater, then went on tour, playing one-night stands in the towns of the interior.

CHAPTER 7

The Battles of
Belles-Lettres

I.

Following its brief literary flowering in the middle and late 1860s—the period of Twain, Harte, and half a dozen others —San Francisco entered into the artistic doldrums, with few writers or painters of importance putting in an appearance for the better part of two decades. Then, with the opening of the 1890s, came a new upsurge of creative talent in all phases of art, one that for the next fifteen years made the town a recognized center of literary and artistic endeavor.

Indicative of this renaissance was the publication in 1893 of a fat little volume bearing the title, *The Story of the Files.* Issued under the auspices of the World's Fair Commission of California, its purpose, according to its author, was to acquaint visitors to the Columbian Exposition then being held in Chicago not only with "the products of California's soil, but also evidences of the culture and industry of her people." The work of a local newspaperwoman named Ella Sterling Cummins—who later adopted the pseudonym of "Aurora Esmeralda," linking the names of two Nevada silver towns where she had lived as a child—the book not only traced the histories of the numerous daily, weekly, and monthly journals then being published in San Francisco, but presented numerous brief biographical sketches of their owners, editors, and star contributors.

Of the scores of names thus mentioned, by far the greater number have long since been forgotten: obscure writers of verse or fiction, the editors and staff members of half a dozen short-lived periodicals, and a long list of others whose works, once widely read, today awaken few glimmers of memory.

There were, however, a considerable number, who, then virtually unknown, were to go on to distinguished careers. One such was Frank Norris, then just past twenty-two and a student at the University of California, whose first book— a tale of derring-do in medieval France, written in rhymed couplets—had recently been published. Another was Gertrude Franklin Atherton, member of a well-known local family, who—over the vigorous protests of her conservative mother-in-law—had determined to follow the "unladylike" profession of letters. Her novel, *The Doomswoman,* published the year previous, had attracted no little attention, and was to be followed during the course of the next half century by two scores of others. Yet another was Kate Douglas Wiggin, nee Kate Smith, locally noted for having founded the first kindergarten in the town and for contributing a number of children's stories to *St. Nicholas Magazine.* Still in the future were her widely popular novels, *Rebecca of Sunnybrook Farm, Mother Carey's Chickens,* and numerous others.

In the field of prosody the work of a young Oakland schoolmaster named Charles Edwin Markham came in for brief mention, he having won first prize in a contest sponsored by a poetry magazine for the best quatrain defining the true field of poetry. His winning contribution was:

She comes like the husht beauty of the night,
    And sees too deep for laughter,
Her touch is a vibration and a light
    From worlds before and after.

Another who was mentioned in passing was a journalist named Edward L. Townsend, whose short stories had been appearing in the local weeklies. Later Senator George Hearst took the reporter to Washington, D.C., as his secretary. Not many years thereafter Townsend became widely known for his "Chimmie-Fadden" stories, humorous tales of a New York street urchin.

Local playwrights, too, came in for mention in *The Story of the Files,* among them Clay Greene, Dan O'Connell, and several others. Only one of these, however, is recalled today: Archibald Clavering Gunther. Gunther, who spent his childhood and youth in San Francisco and there wrote his first plays, presently went on to the East Coast, where he scored a wide popular success with *Mr. Barnes of New York, Strictly Business,* and their successors.

Among many newspapermen who came in for attention was Sam Davis. Before moving on to San Francisco, Davis had been editor of the Carson City *Appeal,* one of the band of uninhibited Nevada journalists that included Mark Twain and Dan De Quille of the *Territorial Enterprise* and Fred Hart of Austin's *Reese River Reveille.* During his stay at Carson, Davis was responsible for two feats that are remembered to this day. One was his sponsorship of an Arbor Day celebration during which hundreds of trees were planted by the school children and others, thereby converting the town's barren site into the picturesquely wooded spot it has remained ever since. His second claim to fame lay in a quite different field; local tradition has it that he was the first to compose and display the sign that became a fixture of gambling houses

all over the West, namely, that above the musicians' stand
reading: "Don't shoot the piano player; he's doing his level
best."

Another figure prominently mentioned in the Cummins
book was Charles Warren Stoddard, who had long been conspicuous in the literary and Bohemian life of the city and
was to remain so for another decade. Stoddard, whose parents
had brought him West as a frail, introspective child of twelve,
grew to young manhood alternately fascinated and repelled
by what he saw in the raw, turbulent town.

Sensitive by nature and with a lifelong distaste for the
dull routine of the business world, he early turned to literature as a means of escaping that fate. As a youth he spent
whatever time he could steal from a succession of uncongenial jobs by writing poetry, brief, sentimental verses in the
manner of the times. One day he screwed up his courage to
the point of dropping the latest of his effusions in the box
before the Clay Street office of a pioneer weekly, the *Golden
Era*. On opening the pages of the next issue he found to his
delight that his contribution had been printed, complete with
the pseudonym, "Pip Pepperpod," he had attached to it, for
he had been too shy to sign his own name.

Thereafter he each week slipped other manuscripts into
the box, all of which were published, and the editor presently
added a note to one praising its quality and inviting the
author to make himself known. About that same time—as
Stoddard himself later recalled—a distinguished-looking
gentleman, Thomas Starr King, pastor of the local Unitarian
church, dropped into the bookshop of Chilion Beach, where
Stoddard was then working, produced a poem clipped from
the *Era* and, having praised it highly, asked the youth if by
any chance he was its author. Stoddard, vastly flattered, admitted the charge, and King, after further compliments, took

his departure, having first presented the budding author with a season ticket to a lecture series he was currently delivering on the American poets.

After that the novice's progress was rapid. Discarding his Pip Pepperpod nom de plume, he set to work in earnest, and his writings, both poetry and prose, were presently appearing not only in the *Era* but in other of the town's journals. In 1867, when he was twenty-four, his *Collected Poems* were published in a handsome little volume produced in the printing shop of Edward Bosqui, with illustrations by a rising young artist named William Keith.

Meantime Stoddard had made the acquaintance of a group of writers who, like himself, were just coming to public notice, among them Harte, Prentice Mulford, Joaquin Miller, John Muir, and Ina Coolbrith. With the founding, in 1868, of the *Overland Monthly*, Stoddard came into his own. From its beginning he, along with the fastidious Bret, and pretty, gracious Ina, presided over its fortunes, forming a tight inner circle that other local writers soon began referring to—not without a touch of malice—as the "Golden Gate Trinity." The three were much together, during the daytime at the *Overland* office on Clay Street and evenings at the Coolbrith flat high on the slope of Russian Hill, endlessly discussing the contents of the magazine and laying plans for future issues.

Stoddard's first contributions to the monthly attracted little notice, but with the appearance of "Chumming with a Savage"—the first of his Sandwich Island sketches—he hit his stride. A year or two earlier the youth had visited a sister who lived in Hawaii, and had been so charmed by the indolent, carefree life of the natives that he became obsessed with the idea of pushing on and exploring the unspoiled lands that lay farther to the south and west.

The successes of his sketches in the early numbers of the *Overland* encouraged him to embark on that adventure, and in the fall of 1870 he set off for Tahiti, where he hoped to support himself by whatever means presented itself while he studied the customs and lore of the natives and prepared to write about them. The venture failed to work out as planned. On reaching Papeete he discovered that no work was available there for a white man. His small supply of cash was speedily exhausted and he was reduced to the status of a beachcomber, living in the grass huts with the natives and sharing their meager food. At length, an eastbound trading vessel having dropped anchor in the harbor, the whites of the town arranged to have the hungry, ragged youth shipped back to San Francisco.

While his South Sea experiences could hardly have been pleasant when he was undergoing them, their hardships were quickly forgotten by the incurably romantic Stoddard. In retrospect the adventure came to seem a wholly delightful return to the verities and ease of a primitive culture. Such, at any rate, was the impression readers got from the sketches he was presently contributing to the *Overland* and other magazines of the day. These, written in an ornate prose well suited to the flamboyant settings he described and the bizarre nature of his themes, were widely admired, and when the sketches were collected into a volume called *South Sea Idyls*, his reputation was established.

Stoddard remained a fixture of the artistic and Bohemian life of the town for many years thereafter, a friendly, capricious, lackadaisical individual who lived in picturesque squalor, surrounded by his South Sea mementos, in a succession of tumble-down houses on Telegraph and Rincon hills and eking out a precarious existence by doing hackwork for local magazines and newspapers. Somewhere along the line he became a convert to Catholicism and, in the late 1880s, took up teaching, first at Notre Dame and then at the Catholic University of America at Washington, D.C. Thus, during much of the 1890s and early 1900s he was in San Francisco only for a part of each year. But he always looked on the city as his home and it was there he returned in his old age. He died at Monterey in 1909, at the age of sixty-five, a nonconformer to the last and one of the strangest figures in the whole galaxy of California writers.

When, as stated earlier, Robert Louis Stevenson paid his first visit to San Francisco in 1879, Stoddard was one of the local literary lights with whom he became acquainted. The friendship that developed between the frail Scot and the capricious, unworldly Yankee was destined to have a profound effect on the future course of Stevenson's career. For, as is well known, it was Stoddard who first stirred the other's interest in the South Seas and aroused in him an ambition someday to visit that then little-known part of the world.

During his earlier stay Stevenson had, despite his poverty and uncertain health, quickly won a place for himself in the artistic and Bohemian life of the town. This had come about mainly because his future wife's daughter, Isobel, had recently married a local artist named Joe Strong and the newcomer was a regular visitor to their studio at 7 Montgomery (now Columbus) Avenue. There the odd-looking but genial stranger met numerous painters and writers, most of whom lived in the neighborhood. Among these were Virgil and Dona Williams, who became lifelong friends. Williams, a painter and art teacher of note, had come West some years earlier and established an art gallery at Woodward's Gardens, a popular amusement resort at Fourteenth and Mission streets. Later he opened an academy of art, the School of Design, which for a time shared quarters with the newly founded Bohemian

Club in rooms above the California Market; Fanny Osbourne and her daughter Isobel had been students there before Stevenson reached San Francisco.

Although Williams was a close friend of Sam Osbourne, Fanny's first husband, he quickly developed a liking for Stevenson. It was on his advice that, after the pair had married, they spent their honeymoon at the abandoned quicksilver mine on the side of Mount St. Helena, and it was to Virgil and Dona Williams that Stevenson dedicated his *Silverado Squatters* when that charming work was published some years later.

The beginnings of Stevenson's friendship with Stoddard came about in a different way. The invalid was in the habit of taking long, solitary walks about the city. One day, having set out to explore Telegraph Hill, he sat down to rest at a point near its crest, and as it happened, directly opposite the ramshackle house in which Stoddard was then living. Thereupon the latter, his interest, as he later recalled, aroused by the stranger's odd attire and general appearance of unworldliness, came out and invited him into the "Plover's Nest," as he termed his rookery. Inevitably the conversation that followed turned to the South Seas—that being the host's major enthusiasm—and when Stevenson left he carried under his arm copies not only of *South Sea Idyls* but Herman Melville's *Typee* and *Omoo*. From his reading of these, and from numerous discussions with Stoddard, sprang Stevenson's abiding interest in all things Polynesian. However, when, some eight years later, he again reached San Francisco, this time deep in preparations to explore that area, neither of his closest local friends, Virgil Williams or Stoddard, was on hand to bid him bon voyage. The painter had died in 1886 and Stoddard was in the East, teaching at Notre Dame.

II.

Looming large on the local literary scene as the 1890s opened, and far overshadowing all other West Coast historians, was the formidable figure of fifty-eight-year-old Hubert Howe Bancroft. The last of his *History of the Pacific States*, aggregating thirty-nine thick volumes, had recently issued from the presses, and after more than two decades of continuous activity his "fiction factory"—as his critics scornfully termed it—was shutting down.

With that phrase "fiction factory" Bancroft had no quarrel; he himself had occasionally used it to describe his methods. He made no attempt to conceal the fact that in compiling and writing his monumental tomes he had employed a large staff of assistants, an arrangement that, in his words, permitted him to assume the over-all direction of the operation without becoming bogged down in a morass of details.

But while its owner was justifiably proud of the smoothly functioning organization he had set up on the top floors of his Market Street headquarters, when his unorthodox history-writing methods first became known they aroused a considerable amount of ridicule. This was particularly so among other workers in that field, historians who, as Bancroft expressed it, produced their works in "antiquated one-man shops."

As time passed, however, such criticisms were less frequently heard. For despite the unconventional methods used in their writing, the big calfbound volumes were found to contain prodigious amounts of western historical lore never before put between covers. Thus although few found their pages sprightly reading—Bancroft and his scribes alike cultivated a dry, pedestrian style of writing—their other virtues came to be widely recognized, and after the first few volumes appeared the critics were for the most part stilled.

But not for long. For beginning in the early 1890s and continuing through most of that decade both Bancroft's methods and the authenticity of his histories were under almost constant attack. One of the first to open fire was a San Francisco lawyer-turned-historian named Theodore H. Hittell, whose four-volume *History of California,* written by the old-fashioned, one-man method, was then under way. In 1891, Hittell stated publicly that Bancroft's history of the state was so unreliable both in its chronicle of past events and in the interpretations put upon them, that he had refrained from consulting them during the preparation of his own work.

Then, in 1893, appeared a second and more devastating blast, this in the form of an eighty-page pamphlet from the hand of Henry L. Oak, a former member of the fiction factory's staff. After some eighteen years there, during which he had risen to the post of chief writing assistant, failing health had caused Oak to resign. Following his retirement he seems to have brooded over certain wrongs, real or imaginary, he had suffered at his employer's hands. The pamphlet that resulted was a curious document. For while, in the main, Oak defended Bancroft on the charges of inaccuracy and bias being made against him, his own attacks were no less bitter, though on different grounds.

The primary cause of Oak's resentment lay in the fact that, although the histories were admittedly a co-operative venture, Bancroft's name alone appeared on their title pages, and nowhere was credit given to those employees—Oak included—who had written by far the greater part of them.

The appearance of the pamphlet aroused widespread discussion, particularly on that last-named point, for there a nice ethical question was involved. Some warmly supported its author's viewpoint, maintaining that if one wrote a book —or had a substantial part in its writing—simple justice demanded that his name appear on it and that he share both the responsibility and credit that might thereby accrue to him. On the other hand, there were those who argued that since Bancroft's collaborators had been paid employees he had a clear right to the result of their labors and could use it in any way he deemed fit. That, incidentally, was the opinion held by Bancroft himself.

Hardly had the furor over the Oak charges subsided when a third and even more violent attack was launched from a new quarter. This, too, was in the form of a pamphlet, issued under the imprint of the Society of California Pioneers, an organization made up of forty-niners and their descendants, which then wielded considerable influence throughout the state. This onslaught was unexpected, for when the first part of Bancroft's history, namely his five-volume *Native Races of the Pacific Coast,* had appeared in the late 1870s, the Society had expressed its approval of that work by electing its author to honorary membership.

However, when *Native Races* was presently followed by an even bulkier work—Bancroft's seven-volume *History of California*—which, with its supplementary volumes, aggregated some five million words—the organization's admiration for its honorary member went into a profound decline. What chiefly aroused the ire of the pioneers and their descendants was the manner in which Bancroft had chosen to treat certain episodes and persons involved in the taking over of the Mexican province by the United States in 1846. For he had sharply criticized the behavior both of Captain John C. Frémont and Commodore Robert F. Stockton during that period, and, in addition, had taken a censorious view of the actions of the band of American settlers who had staged the Bear Flag Rebellion. Although later historians have, in the main, tended to agree with Bancroft's conclusions on both these matters, in the 1890s the Bear Flaggers were looked on as patriots who on all occasions had acted from the highest motives, and Stockton and Frémont—particularly the latter— had attained something of the stature of national heroes.

Holding such views, members of the Society were deeply affronted to learn that Bancroft had termed the glorious coup of the Bear Flaggers "a criminal revolt of vagabond settlers" that had spoiled carefully laid plans for the peaceable taking over of the province by the United States. Even more out- rageous, however, was his calling the heroic Frémont "a fili- buster of moderate abilities" who, by behaving with "foolish bravado," had done "more than any other to prevent or retard the conquest of California."

Accordingly, on December 6, 1893, a message was handed Bancroft directing him to appear at the Society's headquar- ters, Pioneer Hall, six days later and "answer certain charges against you as an Honorary Member of this Society." When Bancroft ignored this summons, as well as several others that were sent him, the organization published its forty-page pamphlet soundly upbraiding "this so-called historian" who "did wantonly and maliciously wrong the old Argonauts"— and proceeded to strike his name from its membership roll.

Bancroft professed to be unperturbed by their action. He had, he announced, not sought membership in the first place and so it was a matter of indifference to him whether or not the Society now saw fit to expel him. Clearly it was that atti- tude, quite as much as the alleged misrepresentations in his histories, that so enraged the Pioneers.

III.

Hardly had the furor caused by Bancroft's expulsion from the Society of California Pioneers died down when the town was treated to a new sensation, this, too, having literary overtones.

In the spring of 1895 appeared a book that, in the words of one of the local journals, "had the effect of a bombshell." This work, while it could hardly be termed a work of art, was on a theme that made it required reading for all San Franciscans who professed to be in the know. Its title was *Chambliss' Diary; or Society as It Really Is,* and its purpose, according to the author, was to "expose the pretentions and absurdities of the new-rich," whom he termed the Parvenucracy. What stirred the interest of the locals was the fact that its writer, a young southerner named William H. Chambliss, had gathered the material for his exposé in San Francisco, and for months rumors had been circulating about town that he had handled the subject in a manner likely to set off a major social explosion.

Some of these stories had reached the nabobs on Nob Hill, where they churned up enough uneasiness to bring about determined attempts to suppress the book. For the author's original plan was to produce and publish the work locally, and contracts had been signed with a San Francisco printing firm to put the text in type and with a lithographer to reproduce the illustrations. Work on these projects was well advanced when the owners of both firms informed him that they would not complete the job. Moreover, according to Chambliss, they refused either to return his manuscript or the originals of the illustrations.

When news of these developments got about, it of course stirred public interest still higher, providing highly valuable advance publicity for the work. The *Examiner* commented: "That there should be considerable dissension from the publication of Mr. Chambliss's Diary, wherein he has unfolded his secrets concerning the personnel of society, is natural; that the dissenters should be persons of prominence in that 'sacred' circle no less so . . ." and went on to prophesy that "neither social distinction, nor obscure origin, nor financial worth" of those about whom Chambliss had written would turn him aside from his purpose of making his findings known to the world.

True to that prediction, the author sued the printer for the return of his manuscript, had the artist make a new set of drawings and, in his words, "determined not to be outdone by the enemies of decent society . . . took the train for New York in quest of an honest printing house." Evidently the influence of the San Francisco "Parvenucrats" was less strong on the far side of the continent, for the book was speedily set up and printed and bound, and an ample supply was hurried out to the West Coast.

While *Chambliss' Diary* was, as has been indicated, something less than a literary gem, in one respect at least—namely, on the score of frankness—it fully lived up to its advance billing. Few of the socially eminent residents of Nob Hill ("Snob Hill" the author termed it) failed to come under the scrutiny of the iconoclast—with results that were seldom flattering. Marriages between the daughters of rich Americans and foreigners of title were both frequent and newsworthy during the 1890s and this provided him with some of his most effective ammunition.

Nor in his search for examples of that practice did he have to go far afield. In 1889 Eva Bryant, adopted daughter of bonanza king John W. Mackay, had married Prince Ferdinand Colonna, bringing to the scion of that ancient but impoverished Italian family a dowry that Chambliss estimated at five million dollars. Soon thereafter the stepdaughter of a second western plutocrat, railroad magnate Collis P. Huntington, was united with a Prince Hatzfeldt, and again, by Chambliss' estimate, several millions of western-produced wealth crossed the Atlantic to bolster the fortunes of one of Europe's effete titled families.

This brace of California maidens who, in Chambliss' words, "had traded their very souls and bodies, as well as their ill-gotten gold, for ignoble empty titles" by no means exhausted the list. Some of the critic's sharpest darts were aimed at yet another international romance with local ramifications: that of Beth Sperry and Polish Prince André Poniatowski. Miss Sperry, member of a well-known family of California flour millers, was a sister-in-law of William H. Crocker, and Crocker was, stated the writer, the acknowledged kingpin of the "Snob Hill" social set.

The fact that Crocker had, according to Chambliss, purchased Miss Beth her title at a bargain-counter price did not change his opinion that the investment had been a poor one. The writer made much of the fact that American Indian blood was said to flow in the veins of the Sperrys, and he professed to regret that the bridegroom had failed to make the most of that circumstance. "If the penniless Poniatowski," he commented, "could only induce his new owner to dress up in the good, old-time American style—the style of her ancestors, so to speak—I think she would make a great hit on the boulevards, and on Fifth Avenue, or even on our own Market Street promenade, where wilderness and wool and papoose baskets are fresh in the memory of men still living in San Francisco." Pursuing that fancy, the author included among the illustrations of his book a full-page drawing depicting the princess wrapped in an Indian blanket, wearing a feathered headdress and, on her back, a wicker basket containing a genially grinning papoose.

Naturally these, together with other none too mild thrusts at the behavior and pretensions of the town's first families, did not endear the author or his book to the socially elect. Having failed to prevent its publication, some of their number sought to accomplish the same end by buying up and destroying copies as fast as they were placed on sale. For years thereafter one Nob Hill matron had a standing order with the San Francisco bookdealers for every copy that came into their hands. It is said that as each was delivered she personally carried it downstairs and tossed it into the furnace. This protracted one-woman campaign in the end had the desired result. Today the offending *Diary* is by no means easy to come by.

IV.

The furors caused by the publication of the Chambliss book and earlier by Bancroft's ejection from the pioneer society were, however, but manifestations of the widespread interest taken by San Franciscans of the period in anything having to do, however remotely, with the literary or artistic life of the town. For the residents in general were well aware of the numerous colony of painters, writers, musicians, and sculptors then active locally, and in the main they were proud of them, looking with tolerance on their frequently unorthodox behavior and even on occasion buying their wares.

On their part, the artists themselves found in the city an environment well suited to their tastes. The result was that all through the final quarter of the century men of talent in many fields were drawn to San Francisco from elsewhere and settled there, some for a year or two, others permanently. One of the first, and most gifted, of this group was the poet, Richard Realf, whose engaging personality, together with the uniformly high quality of his writings, was recalled long after he had come to his tragic end.

This ill-starred versifier had had a singularly checkered career. Born in the mid-1830s in Sussex, England, of humble parents, he had worked during his youth as a farmhand. When he was seventeen his good looks and winning manner stirred the interest of a wealthy woman of the district, who financed his education and took him into her home, where he became a prime favorite with the ladies belonging to the first families of the county. One of these was Lady Byron, who, when Realf was just short of twenty, sent him to one of her Leicestershire estates, where he became a member of the household of its manager, who was Lady Byron's cousin.

It was while there that young Realf met up with the first of the series of misfortunes that were to dog him the rest of his life. For he and the young daughter of his host became involved in a clandestine love affair and, the girl having become pregnant, Realf fled to a distant town. There he was hunted down by his victim's brother and beaten so severely that for a time his life was despaired of. On his recovery, Lady Byron, wearying of her sponsorship of the handsome youth, shipped him off to New York, where he arrived in the spring of 1855.

There he spent some months working in a settlement house in the city's Five Point slum district. Then, late the following year, having been caught up in the all-absorbing slavery issue, he pushed on to Kansas and joined in the crucial fight to make that territory "free soil." His next move was to Iowa, where John Brown was gathering recruits preparatory to embarking on his quixotic plan of invading the South and freeing the down-trodden slaves. Brown, much impressed by the new recruit, appointed him Secretary of State of the government he planned to set up in the liberated territory, and dispatched him to England to raise funds to finance the projected campaign. While on that errand, however, Realf became so deeply interested in the tenets of the Catholic faith that he decided to adopt that religion. Accordingly, on his return to this country he entered a Jesuit college in Alabama, where, after a course of study, he was baptized a Catholic.

It was while Realf was so occupied that John Brown in the fall of 1859 made his assault on Harper's Ferry, as a result of which he was captured, tried, and on December 2 of that year executed, thereby becoming a martyr in the eyes of anti-slavery adherents throughout the North.

Realf's movements thereafter were rapid. Early in 1860 he testified at Washington before a congressional committee investigating the Brown fiasco. Later that year he appeared at a Shaker colony in Ohio and, forsaking Catholicism, joined that cult and became an eloquent preacher of its doctrines. This, too, proved a short-lived enthusiasm. In the summer of 1862, war having broken out, he enlisted in the Union forces, served with distinction throughout the contest and, soon after peace was restored, contracted the first of a series of matrimonial alliances.

His first wife was a Chicago schoolteacher named Sophia Emery Graves, whom he left three months after their wedding to go on a tour of the vanquished South and investigate the plight of the liberated slaves. She never saw him again. The following year, 1866, he applied for admission to the Oneida Community in upstate New York, then widely known for its advocacy of free-love doctrines. Having been accepted, he was on his way to join the colony when, during a stop at Rochester, he met one Catherine Cassidy and promptly went through a marriage ceremony with her.

Soon thereafter, however, his wanderlust reasserted itself and he next turned up in North Carolina, where he was much in demand as a stump speaker for Republican candidates in the election of 1869. In appreciation of these services he was appointed Assessor of Internal Revenue for South Carolina. There his abandoned Rochester mate presently sought him out and—a shortage in his accounts having been discovered at about the same time—he once more disappeared.

He next bobbed up at Pittsburgh, where he quickly won renown for his eloquence as a speaker, delivering temperance lectures and talks on his experiences during the war. There the persistent Rochester lady again caught up with him, this time with an infant son, of whom she claimed he was the father. Realf denied the allegation and applied for a divorce, which was granted him early in 1873. However, the cast-off mate appealed the verdict to a higher court, which reversed the decree and ordered him to contribute to the support of both wife and child.

This, however, was not the end of his matrimonial mis-alliances. For in the mid-1870s yet another young woman appeared who claimed he was her husband and the father of newborn triplets. What disposition was made of that case is not known, but soon thereafter Realf, anxious to put as much distance as possible between himself and his troubles, again lit out, this time heading for the West Coast. He reached San Francisco in the summer of 1878, where his friend, General John F. Miller—on whose staff he had served during the war—was instrumental in getting him a berth in the local mint.

Throughout all his by no means tranquil career he seems to have found solace by writing poetry, and soon a series of notable poems from his pen began to appear in the *Argonaut.* While these speedily brought him to the attention of the local literati, their publication was destined to have a tragic result. For the ever-vigilant Catherine Cassidy thereby learned of his whereabouts and set off in pursuit.

She appeared in San Francisco at the end of October 1878, only four months after Realf himself had arrived. On the day following their stormy meeting Realf crossed over to Oakland, took a room at the Windsor Hotel, spent an evening writing farewell letters to friends, and the next morning was found dead, a suicide by poison. On his bedside table, along with the letters, was the manuscript of what became his best-known poem: three sonnets beginning *De mortius nil nisi bonum*—a distinguished work that was widely accepted as an apology, and justification, of his life and the manner of his leaving it.

Scores of new-found friends and admirers attended his funeral, and by them his memory was kept green for many years.

CHAPTER 8

Renaissance: 1890 Style

I.

For all the town's well-merited reputation as a community of nonconformers, certain patterns of behavior were rigidly followed all through the 1890s, and when summer came the families of solvent citizens joined in a mass exodus to the country. Nor did their vacations consist of a restless hurrying from place to place; that was to come later, with the advent of the automobile and the building of paved highways that made accessible the remotest corners of the state.

In that more leisurely age when guests arrived at the resort of their choice, they planned to stay for the duration, whether that be for a mere two weeks or, more often, for the entire summer. To be sure, in the latter case, paterfamilias took his ease in town for most of that period, joining his brood only on weekends. But the women and children had no choice but to stick it out until it was time to return home.

Because transportation facilities were few and slow and expensive, nearly all the more widely patronized resorts were within a day's travel of the city. Within that area, however, was a wide variety of places from which to choose: seaside hotels and cottages, foothill retreats, mountain camp sites, and health spas. The last-named were particular favorites, for the health-building properties claimed for their waters were widely believed, and there was scarcely a hot spring in the entire region that did not have its hotel, bathhouse, and cluster of cottages.

While many such resorts were to be found to the south and east of the city, they were particularly numerous in the area that lay to the north. The Sonoma and Napa valleys and adjacent Lake County were dotted with them, among the best-known being Seigler, Adams, Mark West, and Skaggs Springs, the Geysers, White Sulphur Springs, Bartlett's, and Napa Soda Springs. These all could be reached by taking a ferry across the bay to Tiburon or Vallejo, thence by railroad to the nearest station, where arriving guests and their belongings were hauled by stage to the resort of their choice.

One of the earliest and most renowned of these health spas was at Calistoga, at the northern end of the Napa Valley. Founded in the late 1850s by the energetic Sam Brannan, and modeled on the popular eastern watering place, Saratoga (after which it was named), Calistoga was for several decades the fashionable vacation spot for prosperous bay residents. But its ornate, begabled hotel eventually burned to the ground, and by the time the 1890s rolled around its place had been taken by another resort in the same area, Napa Soda Springs.

Perched on a foothill ledge overlooking the valley, the Springs consisted of a cluster of white buildings, each ornamented with a profusion of "millwork." The grounds were handsomely laid out with flower beds, croquet courts, and ornate garden houses, and, for those who wished to venture farther afield, a network of paths meandering among the trees of the surrounding hillsides. Besides the hotel, bathhouse, and rows of prim cottages, the place boasted a four-story structure known as the Rotunda, built, as its name implied, in circular form, and surmounted by a glass-enclosed observation platform that stood a full seventy-five feet above the ground.

Napa Soda Springs and other elegant resorts of its type were, however, much too expensive to be within the reach of most of the town's painters, writers, musicians, and workers in other fields of art. Moreover, even among those who could afford the high rates charged at such places—up to four dollars per day for a room and three meals—there were few who would patronize them, most of their number preferring an environment more conducive to creative effort. Thus all during the final three decades of the century one of their favorite vacation spots was the old Spanish and Mexican capital, Monterey, the narrow, crooked streets and crumbling adobe buildings of which then possessed a languorous charm.

As time passed, however, that quaint old town experienced a revival of activity; each year its population grew, new buildings went up, and its once sleepy streets became crowded and noisy with traffic. San Francisco's artists and writers, finding it no longer the congenial spot it had once been, began casting about for someplace where they could live and work in reasonable tranquillity and solitude.

Precisely where that sylvan retreat was to be located was for some time in doubt. At first the foothills behind Oakland were favored, for the setting was dramatic, commanding a wide view of the bay, and it was close enough to the flesh-pots of the city to permit frequent visits. One of the first to establish himself there was Joaquin Miller, who pre-empted his windy hilltop, the Hights, in the early 1890s. Not long thereafter a group that included Jack London, George Sterling, Xavier Martinez, Harry Lafler, and Herman Whitaker, settled lower down on the Piedmont Hills. But the town of Oakland was then growing by leaps and bounds and it was not long before scores of houses sprang up in the neighborhood, engulfing the cottages of the artists and writers and causing their occupants one by one to move elsewhere. London retired to a ranch at Glen Ellen and most of the others returned to San Francisco.

A few, however, including George Sterling, ventured farther afield, putting up cabins on a wooded hillside that sloped down to the sea a few miles south of Monterey, thereby founding what was to become the most widely known artists' colony on the entire West Coast. This new settlement, which presently became known as Carmel—it being close to the mouth of the Carmel River, with the ruined Carmel Mission nearby—grew slowly. Besides Sterling, the original group included Mary Austin, James Hopper, Anna Strunsky, and several painters, all at the outset of their careers. From the first these were determined to preserve the rustic charms of their retreat, and to that end they—and those who followed them—strenuously opposed the introduction of modernity in any of its forms. Gas and electricity were frowned on— kerosene lamps or, preferably, candles being considered more conducive to literary or artistic effort; streets through the forest must remain unpaved, sidewalks were verboten, and commercial establishments of any sort—restaurants, inns, even grocery stores—were interdicted.

Later materialism, masquerading under the name of progress, reared its head, and some—but not quite all—of these prohibitions were relaxed. The result is that the Carmel of today has its bustling business center, complete with hotels, banks, shops (the latter usually spelled "shoppes"), and cocktail lounges. The houses lining its residential streets have gas and electricity and telephones; even in recent years one sees TV aerials sprouting from their roofs. A far cry all this from the primeval utopia envisioned by the town's founders! Yet even in its mundane present evidences of their persisting influence are not lacking: in the absence of curbs or cement sidewalks outside the business area, in the lack of all industry save such handcrafts as weaving and metalworking, and in the fact that the pines and oaks and madrones covering the hillside have been preserved, property owners to this day being obliged to get permission from the town fathers before cutting down a single tree.

It is, however, with the early days of the colony that we are here concerned. As a site for his hideaway, Sterling chose a spot in a grove of pines high on the hillside, with a view of the lupine-covered flats sloping down to the white sands of the beach and the indigo sea beyond. There with his own hands he put up his one-room shack, an altarlike stone fireplace nearby, and—by way of propitiating the gods of the forest for his intrusion—he hung on the trunks of the encircling trees the whitened skulls of cows and horses he had picked up on his rambles over the neighboring hills.

One of the first to join him in his forest Eden was Mary Austin, whose *Land of Little Rain*—sketches of life in the arid Owens Valley country where she had formerly lived— had recently been published. It was she, more than any other of that first group, who convinced staid residents of the Monterey area that the new colony sheltered a nest of eccentric, and possibly dangerous, characters. For Mary, then in her mid-thirties, had an all-inclusive scorn of the conventions of the day. Thus on reaching Carmel she had cast aside the unaesthetic garments of civilization and decked out her short, stocky figure in flowing Grecian robes, and so arrayed she roamed the countryside, often in company with Sterling, his

177

lean, Dante-like face surmounted by an unruly mass of chestnut hair. A truly odd-looking pair!

One of Mary's favorite spots was the ruins of the Carmel Mission. There she spent many hours soaking in the atmosphere of the place, for she was then writing a tale of early mission life, *Isidro*, which was published a year or two later. The living quarters she established in the woods were no more pretentious, or orthodox, than those of Sterling, being a rough wooden structure patterned after the wickiups of the Owens Valley Indians. Her workroom—which she referred to grandly as her studio—was a tiny chamber perched high in the branches of an oak, to which she each morning ascended by means of a rickety ladder. There she did her writing, the little structure swaying alarmingly from side to side whenever a brisk wind was blowing.

Another early recruit was, as stated, Jimmy Hopper, ex-University of California football star, who was soon to win distinction as a writer of short stories. In late afternoons, their daily stints of work finished, the three congregated on the beach below, took dips in the surf, and, having built a roaring fire of driftwood, loafed about for an hour or two, meanwhile discussing, in the words of one early member of the group, "the true meaning of art with a capital A, the themes of the poems and stories and novels on which they were engaged, and the lamentable pigheadedness of editors and publishers."

It was not long until word of the new colony, and of the carefree, unfettered—and inexpensive—life to be led there, got about. The result was that the next few years saw a steady influx of new recruits: Nora May French, talented young poetess who a year or two later was to commit suicide on the beach below, reputedly because of an unhappy love affair; Arnold Genthe, photographer, who once boasted that his bungalow had the only cement cellar in the colony; Grace Mc-

Gowan Cooke and Perry Newberry, fiction writers, and the playwright, Hartley Manners. Artists, too, joined the group, some permanently, others for a month or two during the summers and falls. Among them were Maynard Dixon, Jo Mora, the "cowboy painter," Armin Hanson, who specialized in seascapes, Charles Rollo Peters, Anne Bremer, and Florence Lundborg.

Although Jack London was never a Carmel householder, he was often a visitor during the early years, drawn mainly by his friendship for Sterling and his respect for the poet's kindly but discerning criticisms of his manuscripts. Also present one summer was Anna Strunsky, a dark-eyed, intense, Russian Jewess whose intellectual attainments, no less than her abounding vitality, were much admired by London, and with whom he collaborated in the *Kempton-Wace Letters*, a curious little volume dealing in pseudo-scientific vein with the relations between men and women.

Another temporary resident, though at a somewhat later date, was a freckled, argumentative youth in his early twenties—Sinclair Lewis, then secretary to Grace Cooke, fiction writer, and himself ambitious to write novels. For a time "Red" Lewis shared a cabin with still another literary aspirant, a connection of the Norris family of writers—Frank, Charles, and Kathleen—whose name was William Rose Benét. Others who lived there for greater or lesser periods included Harry Leon Wilson, Martin Flavin, Lincoln Steffens, Jesse Lynch Williams, and indeed nearly every literary figure of importance who came to California during the first two decades of the new century.

The one notable exception was Ambrose Bierce. For the doughty Bierce, after a single visit at the behest of Sterling and an evening spent listening to the opinions, both literary and political, advanced by Sterling's cronies, branded the colony "a nest of anarchists," shook its contaminated dust from his feet, and vowed never to return.

As it happened, Bierce was needlessly alarmed. For while Communism was openly practiced in early Carmel, it was not of a sort that offered any serious threat to the republic. The most conspicuous example of its communal life was the setting up at various points in the woods of small wooden stands, where residents left orders for newspapers, groceries, or other supplies, together with the money to pay for them, and the tradespeople on their daily rounds deposited the articles desired, all without fuss or bother and with no record of the pilfering of either goods or money. Another revered institution was the community bulletin board that for years stood in front of the post office. On it was tacked all manner of information: messages to friends, notices of articles lost or found, invitations to civic or social gatherings, together with bits of verse or brief prose homilies put up for the entertainment and possible edification of fellow townsmen.

II.

One householder during Carmel's heyday as an art colony was, as stated, the photographer, Arnold Genthe, who spent much time there during the decade he remained on the coast. Genthe's life story was a colorful one. Son of a Berlin schoolmaster and destined for a career as a teacher of classical philology, he reached California in the mid-1890s, having been engaged as a tutor to a young son of the Baron von Schroeder. Von Schroeder, who had married a daughter of Peter Donahue, capitalist and railroad builder, lived during the summers at the Hotel Rafael, which was owned by his father-in-law. That big resort, set in a wooded, ten-acre park at San Rafael, had long been a favorite vacation spot for San Francisco's socially elite, and Genthe, then in his twenties and gregarious by nature, found it so much to his liking that two years later, his pupil having finished his preparations for college, he abandoned his plan of returning to Germany and elected to stay on permanently.

One reason for that decision was that he had acquired a camera and become so engrossed in its operation that he had decided to make photography a career. Accordingly, having rented a room in a ramshackle building on Sutter Street in San Francisco and fitted it up as a studio, he embarked on that calling, shrewdly sending announcements to the socially eminent families he had met through the Von Schroeders.

That venture prospered from the beginning. For Genthe was a meticulous craftsman who gave careful attention to every phase of the lighting, dress, and pose of his subjects, all of which was in sharp contrast to the slapdash methods of his competitors. His first clients, uniformly pleased with their own portraits—which somehow managed to emphasize their good points while suppressing those less desirable pictorially —told their friends, who flocked to receive the same treatment. Within a year or two he had become *the* society photographer of the town, counting among his sitters members of virtually all the prominent families on Nob Hill and the Western Addition.

But while photographing the local maids and madams was both pleasant and remunerative—for his fees were by no means low—it was not long before his major professional interest had turned elsewhere. San Francisco's curiously mixed population intrigued him and it became his ambition to make a pictorial record of the types to be seen in its various foreign quarters: Italian, Greek, Mexican, Swiss, Russian, and others. In particular he took to haunting the streets and alleys of

Chinatown. There, carrying a camera small enough to be kept out of sight—for the Chinese were suspicious of the instrument, terming it a "black devil box"—he sometimes waited hours before singling out from the passers-by exactly the type for which he was searching.

Thus, with endless patience, and after much experimentation with the photographic equipment and materials then available, he collected scores of unposed portraits of residents of the quarter: pig-tailed coolies and tongmen and merchants, children at their games, richly clad mandarin women hobbling along on their tiny, misshapen feet, slave girls, and gamblers. Not until the fire of 1906 had wiped out the entire district did the documentary value of this collection come to be recognized. When, several years later, a selection of these were reproduced in *Pictures of Old Chinatown*—with text by Will Irwin—the book made something of a sensation.

Genthe, whose erect bearing and formal manners reflected his Prussian upbringing, moved in the most select circles of the town, a regular attendant at the functions of the bon ton and a frequent guest at their houses both in the city and down the peninsula. At the same time he was an equally familiar figure at the far less formal gatherings of the Bohemians, frequently a member of the groups that nightly gathered at Coppa's, Duncan Nichol's Bank Exchange, and at the studios of the many artists, writers, and sculptors then living in the Montgomery-Washington-Jackson area.

During the early years of the new century Genthe spent much time at his Carmel bungalow, a big, rambling structure built in rustic style of the materials available locally and boasting a studio room that measured a full 30 by 60 feet. That spacious chamber became a favorite gathering place both for residents and visitors and remained so as long as the photographer continued to own it.

Genthe chanced to be in San Francisco on the morning of April 18, 1906. Throughout that hectic morning he roamed the littered streets of the town, taking a series of views of the spreading flames and of refugees fleeing toward points of safety. While he was so engaged, the fire engulfed his studio, destroying all but a few of his thousands of negatives. He promptly opened a new studio at the edge of the burned area and soon had as brisk a business as before. A year or two later, however, he—like so many others of the local artistic colony—left the shattered town and headed for the greater opportunities of the East.

Just how strong was this lure of New York to West Coast writers and artists is indicated by a story told years later by Robert H. Davis, former Nevada and San Francisco news-paperman, who was then editor in chief of the Frank A. Mun-sey group of fiction magazines and nationally known for his sponsorship of beginning authors. During the several years "Bob" Davis had worked on the local journals he had, he related, seen a long succession of fellow staff members quit their jobs and head eastward. Since word drifting back indi-cated that none of these was starving, Davis presently screwed up his courage to the point of following them. Before setting off, however, he prudently borrowed $500—$250 each from local capitalists James D. Phelan and James V. Coleman—to tide him over the first few weeks. This, as events proved, was an unnecessary precaution, for promptly on his arrival he found a berth on Pulitzer's *World.* Two years later he moved over to Hearst's *Journal,* and from there to the Munsey maga-zines.

So many former San Francisco newspapermen, writers, and artists were presently in New York that one of their number, Bailey Millard—who as Sunday editor of the *Examiner* had first given Markham's "Hoe Poem" to the world—conceived the idea of inviting the group to dinner, taking notes of their brilliant conversation, and publishing the result in Hearst's *Cosmopolitan,* which he was then editing. The result was considerably less entertaining than Millard had hoped. Their remarks across the dinner table were neither profound nor scintillating, and when the editor showed his report to Hearst the other forbade his publishing it, remarking that to do so would brand all San Franciscans as insufferable bores.

One of the few of the Carmel group who resisted the blandishments of the East Coast was George Sterling, who returned to San Francisco soon after the 1906 fire and remained there until his death a full two decades later. Sterling's close association with San Francisco's artistic life extended well over a third of a century. Born in New York State, he came West in the early 1890s and went to work as a clerk in the Oakland real estate office of a wealthy uncle, Frank C. Havens. From the beginning, however, the youth—he had just turned twenty—was far less interested in the dull routine of business life than in the activities of the artistic and literary crowd on the far side of the bay and it was not long until he had become a familiar figure at the restaurants, bars, and other resorts where these were in the habit of assembling.

By the mid-1890s Sterling's interest in such matters was already of long standing. As a boy he had spent three years at a Catholic school in Maryland, his father, a recent convert to that faith, having placed him there in the hope that he would prepare for the priesthood. That hope had failed to materialize; however, he had there come under the influence of a Father Tabb, one of the instructors, and from that contact had sprung what was to be a lifelong enthusiasm; namely, the writing of poetry.

Early in his career as a poet, Sterling became an admirer of Bierce, whose "Prattle" column in the Sunday *Examiner* was, as stated, widely read, and who had constituted himself, in his young disciple's words, the West Coast's "Rhadamanthus of letters." The two first met, in 1893, at the camp of Bierce's brother Albert beside Lake Temescal in the hills behind Oakland. There the hero-worshiping youth was so awed by the great man's presence that on learning that Bierce planned to sleep in the open, nothing would do but that he, too, must dispense with a tent. He accordingly spread his blankets nearby and spent a sleepless night on the hard ground.

Such a mark of respect was evidently pleasing to "the master"—as Sterling reverently termed him—for he promptly became the critic's favorite protégé. From that time on every line he wrote was submitted to Bierce for criticism, and the latter—who was notoriously chary in his praise of fledgling rhymsters—lauded his work to the skies, terming him the equal of any of the great nineteenth century poets and the peer of most. Whether or not Bierce's influence on what his pupil wrote was good or bad has long been a moot question, but there can be no doubt that the older man's sponsorship, and his lavish praise of whatever Sterling wrote, did much to hasten his arrival.

The result was that throughout the middle and late 1890s Sterling was one of the town's best-known literary figures, a faithful attendant at the spots where the Bohemians foregathered, and already pointed out to sight-seers as one of the shining lights of the local art colony. Moreover, in those days he looked the part: a tall, gaunt young man with a mop of unruly hair framing a face that bore a marked resemblance to Dante, and who dressed in the loose, shapeless garments— complete with flowing black tie—that were the hallmarks of the artistically inclined.

Sterling's early books, all issued by the local bookseller-publisher, A. M. Robertson, were widely praised, and even, on occasion, copies were bought and read. In the van of the tub-thumpers was always Bierce, who greeted each slim volume with encomiums usually reserved for major works of the masters, and regularly heaped coals of fire on the heads of eastern publishers and critics for their blindness in failing to recognize his genius.

The time presently came, however, when Bierce's friendship for the other cooled considerably, though he continued to the end to praise his poetry. This came about because of Sterling's admiration for the work of young Jack London, whose Alaska stories were then all the rage. For London loudly proclaimed himself a Socialist—a precept that to Bierce's mind ranked with such absurdities as free verse, woman suffrage, and the total submersion—and when Sterling, too, embraced that doctrine Bierce promptly dropped him from his list of acquaintances.

Some years later, however, the strong-willed Ambrose relented and his friendship with Sterling was resumed, but never on quite the old basis. All the while he had refused to meet London, and Sterling on his part was content to keep the two apart, fearing the explosion that would surely result should they ever meet. Then, one summer in the early 1900s when both men were present at the encampment of the Bohemian Club on the Russian River, Bierce, having learned of London's presence, asked Sterling to bring him around and introduce him. When the mild-mannered poet protested that the two would promptly start feuding, Bierce reassured him, promising to treat the other's friend "like a Dutch uncle." Still doubtful, Sterling hunted up London—who was deep in a poker game—and took him to the camp where Bierce was waiting. True to his word, Bierce was affability itself, and at the end of a long and convivial evening Sterling and London set off to see the other home, for Bierce was staying, not at the grove, but at the cabin of his brother a mile or so distant.

To reach the cabin they had to cross the river in a row-boat, then follow the railroad tracks that paralleled its far bank. The stream itself was successfully negotiated, but after Sterling and London had proceeded some distance down the track, both singing lustily, they became aware that Bierce was no longer with them. Retracing their steps and loudly calling his name, they presently heard a weak answer. This came from the bottom of the steep embankment, Bierce having veered off from his companions and rolled down to the water's edge. He was somehow got safely up the bank and the party proceeded without further mishap to the cabin. There Sterling, himself no mean tippler, promptly fell asleep. The other two, however, were made of sterner stuff; they sat up until day-light and during the course of their amiable discussion each, by Sterling's later account, consumed a bottle of Three Star Martel!

Sterling was, as stated, almost the only one of his group who resisted the urge to try his luck in the publishing centers of the East. Except for his few years at Carmel in the early 1900s, San Francisco remained his home for the rest of his days. There he was always the center about which revolved such Bohemian life as existed after the fire, and as time passed, he became a sort of symbol of what the town had been during its literary and artistic heyday. Modest and self-effacing by nature, he wore lightly his honors as San Francisco's premier poet, somehow supporting himself by his verses, saluting each civic event with an appropriate ode, and ever generous in his praise of such new versemakers as appeared on the local horizon. One such was Robinson Jeffers; Sterling was among the first to recognize the high quality of

187

Jeffers's work and he lost no opportunity to make it known to the world.

Throughout his last years the amiable poet was an unfailing source of copy to the town's journalists, who delighted to record—usually in a vein of good-natured hyperbole—the mild escapades in which he continued to get himself involved, as, for instance, the occasion on which he and a young woman companion, after a round of the North Beach bistros, went for a midnight swim in one of the lakes of Golden Gate Park. For Sterling was in truth the town's last Bohemian, the sole remaining reminder of an earlier and more carefree era, and when he died—by his own hand—in 1926 the whole populace mourned his passing.

III.

Two of Sterling's closest friends—although, as we have seen, they were poles apart in their political and social beliefs —were Ambrose Bierce and Jack London. It is curious to recall that all three came to tragic ends, Sterling and London by suicide, and the seventy-one-year-old Bierce disappearing in 1913 into war-torn Mexico.

At the time he dropped from sight, Bierce had not been a resident of San Francisco for more than a decade and a half, having been called East by Hearst in the mid-1890s and thereafter having lived at Washington, D.C., where he seems to have spent a major part of his time fighting over the battles of the Civil War with a group of cronies at the Army and Navy Club.

San Francisco, however, and indeed all California, had by no means forgotten him. Throughout the 1880s and well into the next decade he had been the West Coast's most widely read literary critic, to whose column thousands turned each Sunday morning, eager to learn what he had to say about the current output of the area's poets and prose writers. In this they were usually rewarded, for although "Prattle" was by no means exclusively concerned with literature—much of it being devoted to politics and, as he once expressed it, "kindred imbecilities"—few local scribblers who were so rash as to break into print failed to come under his all-seeing eye. Moreover, so great was the Biercian prestige that once he had rendered his verdict there was virtually no appeal.

Having joined the *Examiner* staff in 1887, Bierce continued his "Prattle," with occasional lapses, for nine years, abandoning it when, in 1896, he went to Washington to spearhead Hearst's fight against the Southern Pacific's controversial Refunding Bill. Before departing on that congenial errand, he had made himself by far the coast's most influential journalist. Constituting himself an omnipotent oracle, and brooking no opposition, he weekly issued his pronouncements on all manner of subjects, but with special reference to the absurd behavior of *homo sapiens*.

Although it was his habit to introduce a topic with the modest statement that he had no special knowledge of the subject, he proceeded to lay down the law in no uncertain terms, and woe betide anyone who ventured to dispute his findings. Thus while maintaining that he was no poet, he did not hesitate to constitute himself the arbiter of what the many rhymsters of the area should or should not write. Moreover, his pronouncements were delivered with a finality that left no room for argument. Let a local poet bring forth a small volume of innocuous verse and the master would pounce on it with gusto, quoting its more banal passages, pointing out its faults of context or treatment, and holding up the wretched author to public ridicule.

But while most of the region's versifiers received such treatment from his hands, there were always a few for whom he had words of encouragement. Foremost among these favorites was, of course, George Sterling, whose *Wine of Wizardry,* among others, he praised to the skies, stating that it had "all the imagination of 'Cosmos' and all the fancy of 'The Faerie Queene.' " But there were others whose poetry he from time to time found worthy of praise. Among them were Carroll Carrington, a crippled youth who worked on an Oakland newspaper, and Herman Scheffauer, student of architecture whose contributions of verse to "Prattle" had attracted the master's attention.

It was this trio, Bierce, Carrington, and Scheffauer, who, in the latter 1890s, cooked up a literary hoax designed both to amuse themselves and hoodwink the public. Scheffauer, when but twenty-one, had written a poem called *The Sea of Serenity,* which in context and meter bore a superficial resemblance to the work of Poe. Bierce had admired the poem and it was at his suggestion that it was run in the *Examiner* as an authentic work of Poe, together with an explanation as to how the manuscript had found its way to that paper. "A relation of the stilled singer," this stated, "now residing in the southern part of California, had cherished in private for many years a few sheets of manuscript which were committed to her keeping direct from his pen . . . The roundabout and somewhat mysterious way in which it came into the possession of the 'Examiner' adds a flavor of extraneous interest which by no means detracts from the charm of the beautiful lines."

If the three conspirators had hoped to stir up a spirited controversy as to the poem's authenticity they were doomed to disappointment. Evidently the *Examiner's* readers were supremely indifferent to the question of whether or not the verses had been written by Poe, and a few days later the paper printed a somewhat lame explanation, identifying its author as Scheffauer and stating that his attempt to palm off his work as that of another was pardonable, "since modesty alone was responsible for it."

Sterling, Carrington, and Scheffauer were, however, not the only local writers who at one time or another enjoyed Bierce's favor. Others included Ina Coolbrith and Emma Frances Dawson the first well known as a coworker with Bret Harte in the early days of the *Overland Monthly,* and the second a writer both of poetry and prose of a high order. Two of Miss Dawson's stories, "An Itinerant House" and "A Gracious Visitation," were widely praised on their first publication, Bierce, in a characteristic passage, stating that "those readers who do not remember them must have minds that are steel to impress and tallow to retain."

Another who briefly won the plaudits of the critic was a young German emigree named Adolphe Danziger, who, educated as a rabbi, had turned first to the law, and then to dentistry. Literature, too, was one of the versatile doctor's enthusiasms and when, in 1891, he rewrote from the German a melodramatic yarn about a monk who murdered his beloved to prevent her marrying a rival, he induced Bierce to edit his translation. The result was published as *The Monk and the Hangman's Daughter,* with both their names on the title page. The book made something of a stir locally. Presently, however, the two collaborators were at sword's point, Danziger maintaining that he alone had written the story, and Bierce in his column aiming his heaviest artillery at his recent friend. One of the mildest of these salvos was his comment that "I never was ashamed of being an infidel until Dr. Danziger assured me that he was one."

From the above—and from any number of like instances— it will become clear that for a writer to find favor in Bierce's eyes did not necessarily mean he would continue to enjoy that distinction. Indeed, the chances were that he—or she—would sooner or later commit some breach of the strict code of conduct the master demanded of his disciples, whereupon he would be cast into the outer darkness. Then, should the luckless wretch venture to write another story or poem or publish another book, his ex-champion could be counted on to blast it with particular enthusiasm. Thus for a writer to be singled out for the Biercian plaudits was—as any number of them learned—no unalloyed blessing.

IV.

Bierce's and London's night-long drinking bout at the Bohemian Grove failed to make them friends. The pair were much too far apart in their thinking to make any common meeting ground possible, and their feud continued, with neither neglecting any opportunity to take pot shots at the other. Thus we find London writing an acquaintance of the journalist that "Bierce would bury his best friend with a sigh of relief, and express satisfaction that he was done with him," while Bierce, in replying to a letter from Sterling in which the poet had expressed concern for London's safety during his projected round-the-world cruise in the *Snark*, stated his belief that the other was exposing himself to no real danger, his reason being that "the ocean will refuse to swallow him."

It has been hinted that the real reason for Bierce's deep-seated animosity toward London lay not in the younger man's extreme radicalism, but in the fact that he, almost alone among San Francisco writers of the day, had come to the fore without having first submitted his work to the master and thus obtaining the potent Biercian seal of approval.

Despite that handicap—if it was a handicap—London's rise was phenomenal. After a poverty-stricken childhood and sundry adventures as a wharf rat and self-styled "oyster pirate," he had become fired with the reformer's zeal, had cast his lot with the working stiffs and proceeded to wage all-out warfare on their oppressors, the "bloated capitalists." In that capacity he, although not yet seventeen, had, in the midst of the depression of 1893 joined one of the brigades of "General" Jacob S. Coxey's ragtag army on its trek to Washington to demand of the lawmakers measures to ease the lot of the underprivileged.

From that fruitless mission young Jack rode the rods back to California, a confirmed rebel and more determined than ever to play a part in the coming war of the classes. To prepare himself for his chosen role he set about to get an education, reading omnivorously at the Oakland Public Library, and there coming under the influence of the gentle poetess, Ina Coolbrith, and the reference librarian, Frederick I. Bamford, both warm sympathizers with the lot of the underdog. His studies directed by these friendly mentors, he, after a few months at the Oakland High School, was able to gain admittance to the University of California.

His stay there, however, was brief, partly because it was a struggle to support himself, but mainly due to the realization that he could better serve the Socialist cause by taking an active part in its battles. Thus by the mid-1890s we find him in regular attendance at party gatherings on both sides of the bay, sharing in their heated discussions and, in the role of boy orator, nightly delivering harangues on street corners denouncing the iniquities of the rich and painting gaudy pictures of the liberation of the wage slaves "come the revolution."

Although his reformer's zeal remained high all through that

period, his main interest gradually veered off in another direction. He had early discovered that he had a knack for putting words on paper, and the publication of several of his stories in the high school and college papers strengthened his resolve to make a career of authorship. For the next several years he industriously pursued both enthusiasms, daily and nightly attending meetings of his fellow Socialists and delivering his incendiary speeches before sidewalk audiences, and between times grinding out a steady stream of stories and articles which he submitted to the editors of local newspapers and magazines.

The furious pace he had set for himself—he later recalled that he had allowed himself but three or four hours' sleep nightly—would have been catastrophic to one of less abounding health and vitality, yet he kept it up for several years and with apparently no ill effects. In the spring of 1897, however, that Spartan schedule was abruptly broken; word that rich gold fields had been discovered in Alaska reached San Francisco, and London made haste to join the rush to the Klondike.

That venture proved a decisive turning point in his career. For while he, like all but a few of his fellow prospectors, found little in the way of gold, on his return to California he discovered that the entire nation was avid for information about the far north. Here was a literary claim waiting to be exploited and London set to with all his abounding energy. Although at first sales were few, they presently became frequent enough to afford him a precarious livelihood.

In 1900, when he was twenty-three and just becoming established as a writer, he married Bessie Maddern, an Oakland schoolteacher and a distant relative of the then well-known actress, Minnie Maddern Fiske. The pair set up housekeeping in a cottage in the hills behind Oakland, and it was there that he produced the works that won him national recognition: his first Alaska book, *The Son of the Wolf,* appearing in 1900, and the highly successful *Call of the Wild* following three years later.

All his life London was gregarious by nature, and during that early period his hillside cottage was a popular meeting place for numerous artists, writers, reformers, and others from both sides of the bay. One of the regulars at these gatherings was Xavier Martinez, who had a studio close by—the exuberant "Marty" whose vivid paintings and no less colorful attire were looked on by staid citizens as Bohemianism personified. For Marty's invariable costume, even on the most formal occasions, was voluminous corduroy trousers, robin's-egg-blue shirt, a crimson band about his ample middle, and a flowing bow tie. Other less resplendent regulars were Sterling and Scheffauer, Bamford, Austin Lewis, attorney and ardent Socialist, Edwin Markham, Anna Strunsky, Harry Lafler, and on occasion Joaquin Miller, who lived higher up in the hills.

Although in his personal relationships London was normally genial and easygoing, he nonetheless had an unshakable conviction of the soundness of his own beliefs and a fierce intolerance of those who held contrary views. Thus in arguments—which he loved—it was his habit to overcome the opposition not so much by a logical marshaling of facts as by the vehemence of his delivery, reducing the other to silence by the very length and volume of his tirades.

Moreover, it made little difference whether the subject under discussion was one on which he was well posted—as, for instance, anything to do with the much-debated class struggle—or one of which he knew next to nothing. The story is told that at a meeting in the late 1890s of Oakland's left-wing Ruskin Club, the speaker of the evening was David

Starr Jordan, president of Stanford University and a world authority on piscatology. During the discussion period that followed, London—whose knowledge of that science was limited to what he had learned on a whaling voyage to the Bering Sea when he was seventeen—took issue with certain of Jordan's conclusions and, in the words of one who was present, stood up and in an hour-long discourse "proceeded to tell the Doctor all about fishes."

After the breakup of his first marriage London moved to Glen Ellen, at the head of the Sonoma Valley, and San Franciscans saw much less of him. However, when, in the spring of 1907, he set off in the *Snark* on his projected world cruise he began work on *Martin Eden,* the long, semi-autobiographical novel that many believe contains much of his best work. In it he presents a picture of the San Francisco he had known a decade or more earlier, notably the plight of the drifters who lived in poverty and squalor "south o' the slot," and of the group of agitators and reformers endlessly discussing the philosophies of Spencer, Haeckel, Saleeby, and other advanced thinkers of the day. In the book, too, is a graphic description of the trials faced by the beginning writer in finding a market for his wares, of Martin's visits to the offices of locally published magazines, and when one of his manuscripts was accepted, of the drastic methods he employed to secure payment for it.

At the novel's close Martin Eden, having at last gained some measure of success, and finding it not worth the long struggle to attain it, sinks into a profound depression and ends by taking his own life—an example that the author himself was to follow some eight years later.

CHAPTER 9

Among Those Present

I.

As the decade of the 1890s opened, there enrolled in the fresh-
man class at the University of California across the bay a
twenty-year-old youth who—understandably enough—stirred
up no little curiosity, plus a certain amount of derision, on
the part of his fellow students. For both in appearance and
manner the newcomer failed by a wide margin to conform to
the conventions of the time and place. A slender, frail-appear-
ing youth, his pale face sporting a wispy mustache and neatly
trimmed sideburns, he had an indubitably foreign look that
set him apart. Moreover, his garments, form-fitting coat,
spats, and brightly colored waistcoat, bore an elegance that
inevitably were looked on as foppish by his less resplendent
classmates. His behavior, too, set him apart, being reserved
and decorous, and even his speech had a preciseness and for-
mality rarely heard on free-and-easy western campuses.

The young man, Benjamin Franklin Norris, was put down
by his fellows as a queer fish, one who, despite his American
name, had the appearance and bearing of a European. That

impression was strengthened by a visit to his room on University Avenue adjacent to the campus, to which he presently invited certain of his classmates. For displayed on the tables and upon the mantel was a collection of objects not often seen in the rooms of Berkeley students of the day. These included a pair of fencing foils, pieces of ancient armor and other souvenirs of medieval France, the prize of the lot being the bones of a human hand ingeniously wired together, with a rusted iron shackle encircling its wrist. On the walls were many drawings of human figures, most of them nudes, which the visitors learned their host himself had done.

Thus it became known that the youth had but recently returned from Paris, where for two years he had been a student at the renowned Atelier Julian, preparing himself for a career as an artist. That, of course, explained his quaint Old World manner and odd attire and indeed made him something of a celebrity on the campus. Moreover, on closer acquaintance he was found to be a high-spirited, fun-loving youth, ever ready to play his part in student activities, particularly in the pranks and horseplay that constituted extracurricular amusements. Hence it was not long before he had become active in student affairs, contributing stories and drawings to the college publications and forming many lasting friendships.

During his four years at Berkeley—he left in 1894, without a degree, having consistently flunked his courses in mathematics—his main interest had shifted from art to literature and a number of his short stories had been published in one or another of the San Francisco weeklies. Upon leaving he went East to Harvard and enrolled in the writing course of Professor L. E. Gates. There he wrote the greater part of *McTeague,* although that famous novel was not published until some five years later. Back in San Francisco in the spring of 1896 he joined the staff of the *Wave,* the weekly to which he had contributed several pieces of fiction while still at Berkeley.

During the nearly three years Norris served as its assistant editor, he wrote a prodigious amount of material for its columns, and meanwhile somehow found time to work and rework the novel manuscripts that by then had become his major interest. Throughout that entire period virtually every number contained one—and frequently several—pieces, signed with either his own name or that of a pseudonymn he had adopted: Justin Sturgis. These included short stories, dialogues, factual articles, interviews, theatrical and art criticisms, editorials, book reviews, and much else—all admirable training for the beginning writer.

In his short novel, *Blix*, published in 1899, Norris gives an entertaining and, on the whole, true picture of his activities and interests during that period, for in it the character Condy Rivers was, as stated earlier, obviously patterned after himself. Rivers, associate editor of the Sunday magazine section of a local newspaper, spent his days and nights hurrying about the city on assignments for his paper, hunting out quaint and colorful phases of its life, and between times busily turning out fiction. "For Condy," wrote Norris, "had developed a taste and talent for writing . . . He had begun by an inoculation of the Kipling virus, had suffered an almost fatal attack of Harding Davis, and had even been affected by Maupassant."

The fiction Norris contributed to the *Wave* included a number of grim happenings on Polk Street, one of the town's neighborhood shopping centers. In them appeared in print for the first time the names of the hulking dentist McTeague and of Trina, his girl friend, for these were incidents lifted bodily from the manuscript of his still unpublished novel, *McTeague*. What impression these powerfully realistic sketches made on readers of the *Wave* must unfortunately be left to conjecture.

In all, close to two hundred of Norris's stories, sketches, or articles appeared in the weekly during his connection with it. Then, early in January 1898, was published the opening installment of a novel, *Moran and the Lady Letty*, which ran through thirteen numbers and ended in the issue of April 9. Although this tale, a story of assorted skulduggeries by land and sea, was assuredly not one of his best, it accomplished what the far more impressive *McTeague* had failed to do; namely, brought its author to the attention of eastern editors and publishers.

While *Moran* was still running in the *Wave*, Norris was summoned to New York, and the novel, after being reserialized in the *Tribune*, was brought out in book form late that year. *McTeague* and *Blix* followed in 1899, and two years later appeared *The Octopus*, the first of his projected three-volume Epic of the Wheat. *The Octopus* firmly established him among the foremost young novelists of the country, a position that he maintained and consolidated until his untimely death, at the age of thirty-two, in 1902.

II.

Norris's departure for New York early in 1898 by no means ended the *Wave's* sponsorship of young writers of promise. Among those just coming into prominence as the century ended, and whose work appeared in its columns, were Will and Wallace Irwin, recent students at Senator Stanford's new university, James Hopper, Gelett Burgess, Harry Bigelow, Frank Bailey Millard, and a long list of others. With Collis Huntington's death in 1900, however, the railroad subsidy that had long helped to sustain it was withdrawn, whereupon the little paper gave up the ghost and its editor, Cosgrave, followed most of his star contributors to New York, where he had a long and successful editorial career.

There was, however, one writer just coming to the fore during that period whose work for some reason or other never found its way into the columns of the *Wave*. That was blond, harum-scarum Gertrude Atherton, born Gertrude Horn, who at eighteen had staged a runaway marriage with a young man named George Atherton, who had been paying ardent court to her mother. The bridegroom was a son of Faxon Atherton, who, having made a fortune in Chile, had settled on a mile-square estate down the peninsula, where he ruled with an iron hand over a numerous brood of sons and daughters. Young Gertrude, willful and fun-loving, did not take kindly to life at Valparaiso Park—as the Atherton place was called —and when her married life presently proved no more to her taste, she returned to San Francisco.

Always an omnivorous reader, she had long toyed with the idea of becoming an author. That ambition was, as we have seen, frowned on by her Castilian mother-in-law, who maintained that writing for publication was no fit occupation for a genteel young lady, particularly for a connection of the exalted Atherton clan. It was, however, not this opposition that had held her back—quite the contrary!—but, as she later recalled, a lack of anything that she considered important enough to commit to paper.

This last-named obstacle was soon overcome. One day, while she was still at Valparaiso Park, she chanced to read a newspaper account of the auctioning off of the belongings of a family that had lived nearby. At once she knew that she had a subject worthy of her best efforts. For the family was that of a once beautiful and accomplished girl named Nelly Gordon, who had been an ornament of San Francisco and peninsula society but, having become a confirmed alcoholic, had literally drunk herself to death.

During the weeks that followed, the embryo novelist locked herself in her room while at fever heat she dashed off a fictionized version of Nelly Gordon's story. When her manuscript was finished she mailed it to the *Argonaut*. Shortly thereafter she was summoned to the office of that weekly, where the assistant editor, Jerome Hart, informed her that they had decided to publish her story as a serial. However, Hart strongly advised her that, since the originals of many of her characters would readily be recognized by San Franciscans, she consent to have it appear under a nom de plume. That was quite satisfactory to the proud author. Pocketing the $150 check handed her in payment, she hurried to the nearby bookshop of Chilion Beach, where she spent most of it on books she thought would look well in the library of a successful novelist.

Nelly Gordon's story made the sensation editor Hart had predicted for it, and its author, secure in her anonymity, spent several pleasant weeks sympathizing with enraged friends who had recognized themselves among its characters, and joining in guesses as to who the culpable author might be. No one suspected her.

That first Atherton yarn was destined to have a curious history. After it had run in the *Argonaut,* she expanded it to book length and submitted it to several eastern publishing houses. These promptly turned it down, novels about alcoholics—particularly well-born young women alcoholics—being considered unsuited to the tastes of fiction readers of the period. Not until years later did the author, who was then living in England, again take up the story. After a complete rewriting it was eventually published under the title, *A Daughter of the Vine*. Even in that later and supposedly more enlightened day its theme repelled many readers. In her old age its author recalled, with obvious pleasure, that the inmates of one British penitentiary had publicly burned the offending work in the prison yard.

While waiting for a suitable theme for her next novel, she, having shunted off her unwanted husband, established herself in furnished rooms in San Francisco, gathered about her a group of artistic-minded friends, and conducted what in *fin de siècle* parlance was termed a salon. There she occupied herself by writing stories and articles for the *Argonaut,* the *Overland Monthly,* and other local journals. However, seeking a wider field, she at length set off for New York, then continued on to Europe, where she spent the major part of her time for several decades. Meanwhile, her next few novels, forerunners of the two score she was to turn out during her long and active life, had appeared, and by degrees she became, on both sides of the Atlantic, one of the widely read fiction writers of her day.

Because many of her stories were laid in California, she returned to San Francisco from time to time in order, as she expressed it, to keep in touch with her milieu. Usually, however, her stays in the city itself were brief, for the place had depressing memories of her short married life, and besides she found the prefire town, with its cobbled streets and miles of closely built, bay-windowed residences, bleak and monotonous.

Nonetheless, several of the novels she produced during that period were written in California, though not within the city itself. When she felt a period of activity coming on, it was her custom to retire to a hotel in one or another of the outlying towns—Berkeley, Los Gatos, Sacramento, even once to the tavern atop Mount Tamalpais—and there isolate herself for months until the manuscript was completed.

One of the most widely read of her early novels, *The Doomswoman*, published in 1892, was written near Fort Ross, the former Russian outpost on the bleak north coast, some sixty miles above San Francisco. Many years later she revisited the little lumbering town hotel where she had spent that stormy winter and asked permission to inspect it. The woman then operating it, unaware of the other's identity, took her on a tour of the sagging structure. Throwing open the door of a corner room on the second floor, she proudly announced that it had once been occupied by two distinguished guests: the novelist Gertrude Atherton and Civil War General William T. Sherman. "But not at the same time, unfortunately!" commented the eighty-five-year-old visitor.

On one of her returns to San Francisco, this time in the mid-1890s, she journeyed to the village of Sunol to pay her respects to Ambrose Bierce, whose Civil War stories, as well as his vitriolic *Examiner* column, she had long admired. Bierce, a sufferer from asthma, found the climate of the bay region uncongenial and accordingly spent most of his time at one or another of a series of resorts farther inland.

The two had never met although they had been in correspondence for some time. By her later account, their meeting at Sunol was not altogether a success. The pair had lunch in the "dreary, fly-specked" dining room of the hotel and spent the afternoon discussing a variety of literary topics. During their talk it was brought out that George Meredith, then much in the public eye, was, in Bierce's opinion, a vastly overrated fellow, while Robert Louis Stevenson was little more than a clever phrasemaker.

Bierce's contempt for these and other popular writers was so extreme that she—although none of those mentioned was among her favorites—felt impelled to come to their defense. Bierce went on to state pontifically that novels were at best an inferior type of literature, not to be compared with short stories. To this heresy his guest retorted that the reason he held that opinion was because he had written only short fiction and knew nothing of the vastly greater problems involved in longer works. She went on to say that all short-story writers were jealous of novelists.

That went on all afternoon, and when it came time for her to catch the train back to San Francisco, Bierce, silent and morose, escorted her to the station. There she relented, telling him that she was sorry she had been so cantankerous and adding that she had long been an admirer of his work, ranking his short stories with the best then being written. Amicable relations having been restored, the pair strolled about while they waited the train's arrival. During their walk they passed and repassed an enclosure in which was confined a brood of squealing pigs. Then, as they were again passing the spot, Bierce suddenly took her in his arms and attempted to kiss her.

Her account of the episode ends thus: "In a flash I knew how to hurt him. Not by struggling and calling him names. I threw back my head—well out of his reach—and laughed gayly. 'The Great Bierce!' I cried. 'Master of style! The god on Olympus at whose feet pilgrims come to worship—trying to kiss a woman by a pigsty!' " The train came in at that moment and, she concludes, "He rushed me to it and almost flung me on board."

The pair never met again, which was perhaps just as well.

III.

All through the 1890s and into the early years of the new century Joaquin Miller, he of the flowing white whiskers, cowboy boots, and resplendent frock coat topped by a ten-gallon hat, was far and away the most picturesque of the bay area's corps of littérateurs. For canny Joaquin was shrewd enough to realize that the public expected poets to be different from the ordinary run of men and, so far as he himself was concerned, he was never averse to furthering that impression. The result was that his carefully cultivated eccentricities both in dress and behavior long made him one of the most widely discussed literary figures of his generation, both in this country and abroad.

There were occasions when his idiosyncrasies of dress were a source of considerable inconvenience for those about him. Once in the early 1890s when he was scheduled to speak before the students and faculty of newly founded Stanford University, as he and President Jordan were about to set off for the lecture hall, Miller informed his companion that he never addressed an audience without a white rose in his buttonhole. This, as Jordan later recalled, presented something of a problem, for the month was December and at that season roses were rare even in California. However, diligent search of the University's botanical gardens turned up a single specimen and the address was delivered on schedule.

Although Miller was normally a man of benign disposition, ever generous in his praise of other writers, for one eminent member of that craft—Bret Harte—he was never heard to say a kind word. The precise reason for his animosity toward the mild-mannered Harte was never known, but several theories have been advanced to account for it. One is that he believed the stories of the California gold towns the other was industriously turning out in England were grossly misleading in that they presented a romanticized picture of life as it had been lived on the Mother Lode. He frequently pointed out that Harte had spent, at the most, but a few weeks in the area, whereas he himself had lived much of his youth in the mountains and hence knew its people intimately and at first hand.

Another and perhaps more substantial reason for his dislike of Harte lay in the fact that when Joaquin had first descended on London, wearing his flamboyant frontier outfit, a bearskin thrown nonchalantly over his shoulders, and proceeded to become the darling of literary-minded hostesses of the day, Harte had not been among those who applauded. In some quarters the other's coolness toward his fellow Californian—which presently developed into open ridicule—was attributed to jealousy of this Johnny-come-lately who was threatening to supplant him as the foremost interpreter of life in the Far West to the British public. In any event, when word of some of the daring personal exploits the newcomer was relating in the London drawing rooms—tales of bloody Indian fights, hairbreadth escapes from stage robbers, and the like—reached Harte's ears, his only comment was: "Joaquin Miller is the greatest liar the world has ever known."

That the normally amiable Miller's dislike of the other was both deep-seated and permanent was demonstrated when, in the early 1900s, he was persuaded to go over from his aerie in the Oakland hills to attend a banquet at the Bohemian Club. He arrived togged out in his usual outfit, complete with bearskin, partook liberally of the food and drink, and remained in high spirits until the speaker of the evening launched into a paean of praise of Harte's early California tales. Thereupon he rose to his feet and stalked majestically from the room. A little later, questions from the floor having been invited, someone asked: "What has become of the old, picturesque Wild West?" and the speaker brought down the house by replying: "Didn't you notice? He just walked out."

Miller's reputation for veracity was never of the highest, a fact that he freely admitted, maintaining that a conscientious artist was under no obligation to spoil a good story by sticking too closely to the facts. "I am not a liar," he once explained, "I merely exaggerate the truth." He long claimed that during one of his youthful clashes with the warlike Modocs he had received a severe arrow wound in the leg, as a result of which he—whenever he chanced to think of it— walked with a pronounced limp. Ambrose Bierce once chided him gently for his faulty memory, pointing out that he had recently taken to limping on the wrong leg.

One of the most widely admired of the poems in his book, *Songs of the Sierras*, which appeared during his stay in London, was a tribute to the Nicaraguan filibuster, William Walker, who had perished before a firing squad. In that elegy Miller wrote in the first person, thereby giving many the impression that he had been a member of the Walker expedition and had been present when its leader was slain. Later when a stranger asked him point-blank if he had really been with Walker in Nicaragua, he replied with dignity: "Was Milton ever in hell?"

Miller's hilltop retreat, the Hights—as he insisted on spelling it—remained the bay area's favorite literary shrine as long as he lived, and those pilgrims who visited the spot felt themselves well repaid. It was, however, not a journey to be undertaken lightly, for it lay several miles from the end of the nearest car line and could be reached only by a winding road that one panting visitor described as "little more than a squirrel's trail." Joaquin's own instructions to prospective callers were simplicity itself. Let them, he stated, make their way to the village of Fruitvale and from that point "proceed three miles east and one mile straight up."

The Hights was an unprepossessing expanse of upland when the poet first settled there in the mid-1880s, its seventy steep acres covered with stunted pines rising out of a tangle of wild blackberry vines and poison oak. However, he lost no time converting it into what he termed a poet's Valhalla, doing most of the work himself although visitors could sometimes be induced to lend a hand. These last were presently fairly numerous, including not only members of the general public but many of the leading literary and artistic lights then living in the area. Joaquin soon discovered, however, that at the end of their long climb his artistic friends were far more interested in slacking their thirst than in wielding a pick or shovel or trundling a loaded wheelbarrow. Accordingly, although he was himself no mean trencherman, he decreed that none of his plentiful supply of spirits—which he kept in five-gallon demijohns—would be dispensed before twelve o'clock noon, an edict that his parched friends grumblingly termed "Joaquin's law."

In spite of that rule—or perhaps because of it—the Valhalla its owner had envisioned gradually took shape. It was an extraordinary conception, one designed to puzzle and bemuse all who laid eyes on it. First to be finished was the poet's combination studio and living quarters, a small chamber made of rough boards, with a high-peaked roof, its floor covered with bearskins and its walls with bows, arrows, tomahawks, and other mementos of his frontier youth. This he termed the Abby, some say in honor of his wife Abigail—from whom he had long been separated—and others that it was named for Newstead Abbey, the ancestral Nottinghamshire seat of his admired Lord Byron.

This, however, was but the beginning. His next project was to beautify the area adjacent to the Abby by erecting there monuments to the memory of three historical personages whom he held in high esteem: Robert Browning and John C. Frémont—both recently deceased—and the prophet Moses. The Browning tribute took the form of a stone tower; that to

Frémont was a single pillar of stone, while Moses's memorial was a rock tomb, shaped—as was meet—in the form of a pyramid. When one visitor inquired if Moses was indeed buried beneath that pile of rocks, Joaquin replied, logically enough, that since no one could say for certain where the prophet lay, it could as well be there as someplace else.

The most renowned of the monuments to be seen at the Hights was, however, the poet's own funeral pyre, a stone platform ten feet high which he had constructed entirely with his own hands, firmly refusing offers of help from friends, and leaving orders that on his death he was to be cremated there and his ashes scattered over the surrounding hillsides. This wish, however, was not to be granted, as we shall presently see.

During all but the last few months of his stay on the Hights, Miller's wife and his daughter, Juanita, continued to live in the East, the former having refused to have any part in his outlandish poet's Valhalla. During the major part of that period, however, he was not without the solace of female companionship. For Joaquin, as he himself was never loath to admit, had a way with the ladies. Just what was the secret of his attraction to members of the opposite sex—irrespective of their age, marital status, or degree of worldly experience— was long a mystery even to his closest friends. To be sure, he was then a literary celebrity of considerable magnitude, and many women who visited the Hights did so to pay their respects to an admired poet.

Although such callers could always be sure of a hospitable welcome, there were occasions when the poet was not above taking measures to speed them on their way again, particularly if they chanced to be neither young nor good-looking. Thus when a delegation from the Oakland W.C.T.U. appeared one day and a stern-visaged member asked what had inspired him to write his celebrated poem, *Columbus,* Joaquin lifted an imaginary goblet to his lips, drained its contents, and replied: "Whisky, madam. Whisky!" Other ladies were, however, more graciously received, and there is record of their having returned again and again; some indeed were known to have taken up semipermanent residence there.

During his last year or two he was joined by Abigail and Juanita, who remained with him to the end. When he died in 1913, it was learned that the Hights had recently been included in the Oakland city limits, and that informal cremations such as he had planned were prohibited by one of the town's ordinances. His friends, however, did their best to carry out his wishes. After his body had been reduced to ashes at an authorized crematorium, the urn containing them was placed on the pyre, a fire was kindled which burned until the metal had melted, whereupon the winds carried the embers off toward the crest of his beloved hills.

IV.

Long one of the faithful hangers-on at literary gatherings on both sides of the bay was Edwin Markham, ex-cowhand and day laborer who had turned pedagogue and, during the mid-1890s, was living in the foothills a half mile or so below Miller's Hights and serving as principal of one of the Oakland schools. As an embryo poet, Markham affected a flowing beard, and he was much pleased when, sitting for a portrait by Arnold Genthe, that artist produced a likeness that not only bore a close resemblance to Longfellow but had overtones suggestive of Walt Whitman.

Although Markham, a facile writer, had been producing verses at a prodigious rate for many years, none of those that found their way into print attracted any particular attention. The consequence was that throughout most of the 1890s his name remained unknown to the general public. As the decade neared its close, however, he published a work that in a matter of weeks catapulted him from obscurity to national fame.

The story of how that near miracle came to pass was repeated for years afterward. At one of San Francisco's literary soirees, this one a New Year's party in the rooms of Carroll Carrington, Markham read a recently completed poem. This one, he explained, had been inspired by a painting of Jean François Millet, which was locally owned by the Crocker family and was currently on display at the Hopkins Art Gallery atop Nob Hill.

Among Carrington's guests was Bailey Millard, Sunday editor of the *Examiner*. Millard was so impressed by the poem —which its author had given the title *The Man with the Hoe,* the same name by which the painting was known— that he asked permission to print it in the paper. It duly appeared in the issue of January 15, 1899, where it occupied the better part of a page. Accompanying it was an editorial note proclaiming it one of the great poems of the generation and adding that its publication heralded the advent of "a new and grand voice, deep-toned and sonorous."

Moreover, the "Hoe Poem"—as it came to be known— fully lived up to its advance billing. It was promptly reprinted in papers from coast to coast, often with editorial comment bearing not only on its literary quality but on its sociological implications. For the pros and cons of Socialism were then a subject of lively, and usually acrimonious, debate all over the country, and Markham's portrayal of the Millet peasant as the brutalized victim of generations of poverty and oppression added fuel to the controversy. It was, of course, greeted with delight by the poet's fellow Socialists, no less an authority than Jack London pronouncing it an inspiring call to arms in the coming war of the classes.

But there were also those who held contrary views, and they, too, were not slow to make themselves heard. One of the earliest of these counterblasts was, surprisingly enough, in the columns of the *Examiner* itself. On the Sunday following its appearance Bierce turned his heaviest guns on the poem's theme, terming as "silly" its contention that the lot of Millet's peasant was due to selfishness or inhumanity on the part of others, and concluding with this blast: "As a literary composition it has not the vitality of a sick fish."

Not long thereafter Bierce found his opinion of the poem upheld in a quarter that must have surprised him: by none other than his archfoe, Collis Huntington, whose Funding Bill, then before Congress, the journalist had been fighting tooth and nail. Granting one of his infrequent interviews, Huntington stated that a man who possessed a hoe, and was thus able to do useful work in the world, was deserving of felicitation rather than commiseration, and went on to announce a prize of $750 for the best poem "answering" the Oakland teacher's dangerous and demagogic doctrine.

At once hundreds of rhymsters all over the nation, spurred on either by their inner convictions or by their hope of carrying off the prize, sprang to the defense of the capitalistic system, turning out so many reams of copy that several months passed before the judges were able to announce their decision. The award finally went to a Chicago poet named John Vance Cheney for a work entitled *Responsibility*. While all that was going on, further fuel was added to the controversy by the pacifists, one eminent spokesman for whom, David Starr Jordan, delivered a series of lectures attributing the "Hoe man's" deplorable condition not to economic or political injustices, but to man's greatest scourge, war.

Thus *The Man with the Hoe* became the subject of lively debate all over the country, and it has been said—with considerable truth—that no poem, or poet, had ever before or has ever since been launched with a greater splash. The *Examiner,* of course, lost no opportunity to compliment itself on its enterprise in having given the great work to the world. Some years later, however, when the paper's owner, having been elected to Congress from New York, began to aspire to the presidency, he had cause to regret having been the means of popularizing it. For a vitriolic parody of the poem—title: *The Man with the Dough*—was widely circulated by his political enemies, thereby seriously damaging his chances. Thereafter fewer references to Markham's *chef-d'oeuvre,* appeared in the columns of the *Examiner.*

Soon after the publication of his renowned poem Markham moved to New York. For the remainder of his long life—he died in 1940—he had the distinction of being one of the few Americans who supported himself by his poetry alone. His successive books sold far better than such works usually do, and his income from that source was supplemented by annual lecture tours and by the sale of his verses to magazines.

It is said that when he submitted a poem to a periodical it was invariably accompanied by a letter fixing the price at which it was offered, and that he steadfastly refused to accept any less. It was his habit, too, to make handwritten copies of his best-known poems and sell them to collectors and other admirers; hence, manuscript versions of such favorites as *The Man with the Hoe, Columbus,* and *Lincoln* are frequently encountered today. On his lecture tours he made a point of visiting the bookshops at each stop and offering to sign copies of any of his books in stock, his charge for that service being one dollar for a simple autograph or, if a line or two of verse was added, twice that sum.

For, unlike most of his fellow verse writers, Markham was a lifelong advocate of applying business methods to the marketing of his wares. As such he deserves—but probably will never get—the gratitude of all members of that notoriously unenterprising craft.

V.

Another widely known member of the town's literary coterie was Ina Coolbrith, she of the classic profile and frank gray eyes, who had been the friend and coworker of the group of young men—Harte, Twain, Stoddard, Miller, and half a dozen others—who had come to the fore during the 1860s and 1870s. She had reached San Francisco during Civil War days and, though still in her early twenties, with something of a reputation as a poetess, her austere, graceful verses having appeared in daily and weekly journals about the bay and in the southern part of the state.

Throughout her long life—she died in 1928 at the age of eighty-five—she wielded an influence on western letters that went far beyond her own writings. For she had the faculty of gathering about her young men and women of talent and by tactful, sagacious counsel spurring them on to their best work. That she was, particularly during her earlier years, a charming and stimulating companion—as well as an uncommonly pretty one—is testified by all who came in contact with her. Her local friends knew her as "Miss" Coolbrith, and although through the 1870s and later she was often rumored to be engaged to one or another of the group that frequented her Russian Hill flat, she remained to the end—so far as the world knew—unmarried.

It was presently revealed, however, that that was not the

case, though it was not until after her death that the story of her marriage came to light. For she herself always maintained a discreet silence concerning her early life. About all she permitted to become known was that she was born in Illinois and had come West in 1851, a member of the emigrant train that had been the first to cross the Sierra over the Beckwourth Pass. What she failed to relate was that her true name was Josephine Smith, her father being Don Carlos Smith, younger son of Joseph Smith, founder of the Mormon Church. Don Carlos, in 1836, had married Agnes Coolbrith, one of the converts who had flocked to the headquarters of the new cult at Kirtland, Ohio; he had died some three years later, shortly after the colony had moved farther west to Nauvoo, Illinois.

His widow, with her three young daughters, had remained at Nauvoo until the sect, by then under the leadership of Brigham Young, had set off for Great Salt Lake. Thereupon, she, weary alike of persecutions from without and dissension within the fold, withdrew. She made her way to St. Louis, where she presently married a man named William Pickett and with him traveled overland to California, settling in the sleepy town of Los Angeles.

The ten-year-old girl—who was soon to discard her real name and adopt that of Ina Coolbrith—accompanied them on the trip. Then, at seventeen, she married a Los Angeles youth named Robert Carsley. This proved an unhappy union and ended in divorce some three years later. It was shortly after she regained her freedom that she appeared in San Francisco.

If her ill-starred marriage had left any scars, she succeeded admirably in concealing them, for her new friends found her an ever-cheerful, high-spirited companion. During the heyday of the *Overland,* she was, as stated earlier, one of the inner group that directed its destinies, and when—after Harte left

216

for the East Coast—the magazine went into a profound decline, she secured a berth as librarian of the Oakland Public
Library.

It was while there that she befriended the young Jack
London, encouraged his habit of voracious reading, and
strove to direct it into fruitful channels. The odd friendship
between the gracious woman and the boy extended over several years, during which he visited the library almost daily,
carrying away as many as a dozen books at a time. These he
raced through greedily, often spending entire nights over
them, propped up in bed at his stepfather's West Oakland
shack or on board the sloop, *Razzle Dazzle,* moored in the
nearby estuary.

At first young London's preference was for tales of action
and adventure, for sea stories and factual accounts of experiences in the far corners of the world. Gradually, however,
under his mentor's guidance, he turned to more substantial
fare: the novels of Herman Melville, Flaubert, and Tolstoi,
and, along with them, weighty tomes on philosophy and eco-
nomics, particularly those dealing with the plight of the
underprivileged and the rise of that new panacea for society's
ills, Socialism. In later years London's path and that of Ina
Coolbrith—who was to survive him by a dozen years—rarely
crossed, but he never failed to give her credit for having
helped open to him the wonders of the printed word.

Another writer of the period, widely known during his lifetime but now almost completely forgotten, was W. C. Morrow, a tall, spare southerner who gave over his days to com-
posing travel folders and other promotional literature for the
Southern Pacific Railroad and his evenings to writing an impressive group of short stories, most of them on bizarre and
gruesome themes. But for all his liking for the melodramatic
in his tales, his treatment of them left little to be desired,

they being told in a clear, limpid prose and with a full appreciation of the psychology that motivated the behavior of his characters.

One of the less grisly of his yarns was "The Ape and the Idiot," in which Romulous, an anthropoid ape, breaks out of its cage in a circus traveling down the Santa Clara Valley and helps a mentally retarded youth escape from a nearby asylum. Freed from the tyranny of their common enemy, man, the pair spend a carefree afternoon, during which they dig up and restore to its Chinese mother a baby who had been prematurely buried before they are captured and returned to servitude. This bitterly ironical tale of protest against man's treatment of such beings was widely read—and hotly debated —when it was first published in 1897. Morrow later conducted what are said to have been the first classes in fiction writing ever held in San Francisco. Among his students were a number who were to achieve a degree of success in that field, the best known of the group being Charles Caldwell Dobie.

Closely akin to Morrow in his choice of themes was William H. Rhodes, who wrote under the penname of "Caxton." Also a southerner by birth, Rhodes practiced law in San Francisco from the mid-1850s onward, but his real interest lay in literature and he was a frequent contributor of verse and prose to local journals. His short stories dealt mainly with pseudo-scientific subjects, usually with overtones of violence. Of his many tales in that vein only one is remembered today: an account of a mad scientist who hit on a means of destroying the world. "The Case of Summerfield" was told with such a wealth of realistic detail that when it first appeared in a local newspaper many readers accepted it as an account of an actual happening, and much uneasiness resulted until its true nature was made known. The yarn has several times been reprinted in recent years.

CHAPTER 10

Brush, Pen, and Chisel

I.

Although more artists of distinction were living in San Francisco during the 1890s than at any other period of its history, few of these were widely known even to the local art fanciers, and in general their sales were few and far between. The reason was not that the town lacked picture buyers; indeed, it was a time when the possession of at least one or two authentic "oil paintings" was looked on as a *sine qua non* in homes of any claim to elegance, as visible evidence of the taste and discrimination of their owners. The result was that not alone did the pretentious homes of the Nob Hill plutocrats each have its art gallery but thousands of prim Victorian parlors on the lower slopes of the hill, along Van Ness Avenue, and in the fast-building Western Addition, boasted that mark of distinction—usually a portrait or a landscape, in an ornate gold frame, hanging above the mantel.

A majority of these showpieces were of European origin, having been acquired in Paris, Rome, or Dresden during their owners' grand tours of the Continent. Others had been bought from one or another of the two leading local art dealers, S. & G. Gump and Vickery, Atkins & Torrey, both of which did a brisk business in the works of then popular—and now forgotten—European artists. Locally produced paintings were, however, by no means overlooked. Why, then, it might be asked, did the town's group of highly competent artists have so much trouble finding buyers for their wares?

The answer to that question is simple. One San Francisco painter so far overshadowed his confreres in public esteem that for all practical purposes he had the field to himself. The man who occupied that enviable position was, of course, William Keith, the canny Scotch emigrant who had arrived during Civil War days, had worked briefly as an engraver, and in the early 1870s—after a year of study at Düsseldorf— had opened his first San Francisco studio in the Mercantile Library Building at Bush and Montgomery streets.

His choice of that location—well removed from the Bohemian quarter at the other end of Montgomery Street—is of no little significance. From the beginning Keith was a staid businessman-artist, spending long hours daily at his studio and having no truck with the improvident, fun-loving painters, sculptors, and scribblers who nightly congregated in the cafés and bars on the lower fringes of Telegraph Hill. Keith's friends and associates were all substantial citizens: bankers, lawyers, prosperous merchants, professors, and the like.

A prodigious worker—he sometimes completed as many as three paintings in the course of a single morning—he was also a highly accomplished salesman and few of the prospective customers who dropped into his studio left without making a purchase. One patron who was particularly useful in spreading abroad his renown—and so stimulating sales—was Collis Huntington. Huntington, whose financial acumen was universally respected—and for good reason—maintained that Keith's landscapes were not only highly decorative but were sound investments as well, and his often repeated advice to friends to "Buy Keiths" was usually followed.

The story is told that so brisk was the demand for Keith's paintings, and so substantial the prices they brought, that the artist presently found himself possessed of a considerable sum for which he had no immediate use. He accordingly asked the advice of one of his financially wise friends as to how he should invest it. The other, William F. Herrin, head of the Southern Pacific's legal staff, replied promptly: "Buy Keiths!"

While he occasionally painted portraits and, on his periodical trips abroad did a number of views of European scenery, by far the greater part of his output were interpretations of the pastoral beauties of his adopted state. The typical Keith landscape showed a tranquil meadow, bordered by clumps of wide-spreading valley oaks, with usually a stream meandering down its middle, an expanse of cloud-flecked sky above, and, in the distance, a succession of straw-colored hills. Rarely were human figures introduced into the compositions, although a few cows were sometimes visible in the middle foreground, placidly grazing on the tall grasses of the meadows.

One characteristic feature of his landscapes was a shaft of light penetrating between the foliage of the overhanging trees and forming a little pool of brightness among the shadows below. The story is told that one day an out-of-town artist called at the master's studio and was hospitably shown a number of recently completed works. After duly admiring them the visitor, striving to be helpful, remarked: "Mr. Keith, I'm going to send you a bottle of a certain chemical I use; I'm sure it will take out those white spots in your paintings,

and without damaging the canvas." What reply—if any—
Keith made has, unfortunately, not been preserved.

Of their sort, his paintings were of a high order of merit,
for Keith was ever a competent craftsman, and although
their quality was uneven—particularly during his immensely
productive middle years—few were downright bad. One of
his closest friends was his fellow Scot, John Muir, and each
summer for many years he spent several weeks in the other's
company on rambles through the canyons and lofty, flower-
strewn meadows of the Sierra. But although in his younger
years he tried his hand at depicting the scenic grandeur of
the mountains, he felt more at home with the tranquil scenery
of the valleys and foothills and thereafter he devoted himself almost exclusively to such subjects.

For many years he lived at Berkeley, a block or two south
of the university, and many of the most admired of his
paintings depicted the venerable oaks on the lower campus.
Keith, however, made no secret of the fact that he presently
grew so familiar with his subject matter that he no longer
had need to paint directly from nature. Thereafter by far
the greater part of his work was composed and executed in
his studio.

In 1894 he moved to larger quarters at 424 Pine Street,
occupying three rooms above the California Market, part of
the space that had recently been vacated by the Bohemian
Club. The first of this three-room suite became his workroom;
the other two were galleries for the display of his paintings.
He was then at the height of his vogue, his clients numbering
—among many others—Charles and Frederick Crocker, James
Flood, John W. Mackay, Mrs. Leland Stanford, Mrs. Mark
Hopkins, Phoebe Hearst, and Henry T. Scott.

Throughout that period the method of acquiring a Keith
was a solemn one, bearing little resemblance to an ordinary

business transaction. One purchaser was so impressed that years later he vividly remembered the experience. On entering the studio he had found the artist at work in the big outer room, and to all appearances so absorbed as to be unaware of the other's presence. After a period which the caller estimated to have been at least ten minutes, he had approached and made known his errand, whereupon the painter had laid down his brush and gravely led the way into the adjoining room.

Across one end of that chamber were a pair of black velvet curtains, behind which Keith stepped briefly, then reappeared and silently drew the curtains apart, revealing one of his landscapes on an easel, brilliantly illuminated by concealed lights. Having given the other several minutes in which to admire it, the artist drew the curtains, substituted another picture, and the process was repeated. Not a word was spoken during this ritualistic procedure until at length, having been privileged to see an even dozen canvases, the impressed caller made known his preference and asked its price. On being told the figure—$300—he counted out that sum and with his picture, carefully wrapped by Keith, under his arm, made his way to the shop of S. & G. Gump to have it suitably framed.

Keith's Scotch thrift was not shunted off even during his years of prosperity. Rain or shine, he walked both ways between the ferry and his studio, and he habitually ate his lunches perched on a stool before one of the counters in the California Market downstairs. His one extravagance was cigars, of which he is said to have smoked half a dozen each day. Even there, however, he was not out of pocket, for he cannily removed the wooden tops from the boxes and made miniature paintings on them.

Although he himself rarely went out socially, one of his close friends, the geographer, George Davidson, was an indefatigable diner-out. Himself a nonsmoker, Davidson was in the habit of passing on to Keith the cigars tendered him by his hosts. It was long a source of wonder to him that the artist, after lighting up and taking a puff of two, could invariably tell at whose house Davidson had been entertained the evening before.

Keith's virtual monopoly on picture sales to local buyers was, not unnaturally, a source of annoyance to his fellow artists, particularly so in view of the fact that he would have no dealings with them, neither joining their associations nor frequenting their gathering places. Some of the group, however—their identity was a closely guarded secret—got a measure of revenge for his standoffishness by concocting a plot that not only caused him much bother but a considerable financial loss. This was none other than the production of a number of spurious Keiths, closely imitating his subjects and style and so skillfully done as to deceive even the experts. In their nefarious scheme the plotters were much aided by the fact that Keith seldom signed his paintings; hence when word got about that counterfeits had appeared on the market there was a sharp dropping off in the sale of the genuine articles.

A far greater catastrophe, however, was the 1906 fire, which destroyed his studio, and, along with it, all but a few of the hundreds of paintings and sketches stored there. The indomitable Keith, though he was then close to seventy, at once set to work, producing a steady stream of new paintings, first at his house in Berkeley, then at the San Francisco studio he presently opened on California Street just beyond the burned area. Although the quality of his work during that period—as well as its quantity—compared favorably with that turned out in prefire days, the long hours spent at the easel overtaxed his strength and his health began to fail. Soon the daily trips across the bay had to be abandoned and, in 1910, his last studio, located at 220 Post Street, was closed.

He died the following year, bringing to a close a career that in many respects was unique among the painters of the West.

II.

Throughout the 1890s in San Francisco, as elsewhere throughout the nation, the one place above all others where tyros with a knack for drawing could most quickly pick up the experience necessary to launch themselves in that profession was the lithography shop. There were, moreover, a dozen such establishments then active in the city, which did the lion's share of all such work being produced on the coast: labels for the containers used by the fruit canners and other food processors, pictorial calendars, show cards, advertisements, multisheet billboard posters, and much else.

To design and execute these varied commissions, each firm had its corps of "artists." These were mostly young men—and women—recruited from the art departments of the local schools, who were hired for brief probationary periods, at the end of which the proficient were retained and the others let out. It used to be said that a year or two in one of these plants was all any artist needed to learn the rudiments of his craft, and the number of such graduates who later became well-known painters, cartoonists, or illustrators seems to bear out that statement.

Another fertile field for the training of competent workers was the art rooms of the town's newspapers. For through the 1890s and into the early years of the new century the reproduction of photographs by means of halftones was far less widely practiced than it later became, and many of the illustrations were still being hand-done.

Here, too, as in the shops of the lithographers, members of

the staff were expected to turn their hands to a great variety of subjects. Thus in the course of a single day the newspaper artist might be assigned to sketch the details of a street accident, picture the bride and groom at a society wedding, and, come evening, provide the sports page with views of a prize fight, a wrestling match, or a six-day bicycle race. It was by no means a life of ease, but the beginner who could stand the long hours and the pressure under which he had to operate seldom failed to develop the knack of doing fast and accurate work.

When young Hearst took over his father's moribund daily in 1887 and proceeded to make local journalistic history by gathering about him a staff of unprecedented size and talent, the *Examiner's* art room became the training ground for a group of cartoonists and illustrators who were later to become nationally known.

One of these was a lanky youth named Homer Davenport, a native of Silverton, Oregon, who, having run away from home and joined up with a one-ring circus, had traveled down the coast to San Francisco. There, having grown tired of caring for the show's one elephant, he applied at the *Examiner* office for a job as a staff artist. The drawings he exhibited, pencil sketches of animals, especially horses (for which he had a lifelong enthusiasm) were crude, for he was entirely self-taught; yet they displayed so much natural ability that he was promptly put to work.

During the next several years the pages of the *Examiner* were almost daily enlivened by drawings from his pen. All were vividly set forth, for he had an uncanny knack of catching in a few deft strokes the movement and drama of whatever he was sent out to portray. As time passed, his work came to occupy ever more important positions in the paper; thus he was presently doing cartoons that appeared on the editorial page or as front-page features. Among his favorite targets were politicians, devastating lampoons of whatever individuals the paper was currently opposing, local bosses and officeholders, railroad magnates, social climbers, and a long list of quacks and charlatans then in the news.

Davenport's technical skill developed so rapidly that within two years after he joined the *Examiner* staff he was widely hailed as the most gifted—and influential—of the town's by no means mediocre corps of newspaper artists. He had, however, one weakness that he was never able to overcome; namely, spelling. The story is told that one day he was at work on a cartoon for the editorial page: a drawing showing the paper's favorite *bête noire*, Huntington, dressed as a nursemaid, holding an infant in his arms and proffering it a nursing bottle. The baby was labeled "California" and it was Davenport's intention to designate the contents of the bottle "Soothing Syrup." Having carefully lettered the first word on the bottle, he was assailed by doubt as to how to spell "Syrup" and asked help from a fellow-artist seated next to him. The other supplied the answer, then was curious enough to step across to see how Davenport had made out with "Soothing." He had spelled it "Suthin."

When in the mid-1890s Hearst bought the New York *Morning Journal,* Davenport was one of several *Examiner* men he took East with him. There for the next decade and a half— he died in 1912 at the age of forty-five—Davenport stood at the top of his profession, his portrayals of Mark Hanna, Teddy Roosevelt, William McKinley, Huntington, and a long list of others, including such symbolic figures as "Uncle Sam" and "The Trusts," becoming familiar to newspaper readers all over the nation.

Another of Hearst's galaxy of future stars was James Swinnerton, later a landscape painter of note, who, while serving his apprenticeship on the *Examiner,* created the mischief-making "Little Jimmie," known to several generations of comic-strip readers. Yet another was "Bud" Fisher. Fisher, sent one day to sketch the habitués of the old Ingleside Race Track, returned with a drawing of an elongated, chinless individual to whom he gave the name of Jeff. The dolorous Jeff reappeared from time to time in later drawings; it was not, however, until his creator gave him a side-kick in the person of a roly-poly, incurably credulous innocent whom he called Mutt that the sketches began to attract attention. Once started, though, they swept the counry like wildfire, their antics appearing in scores of papers, and the name of the smaller of the pair winning a permanent place in the language as a synonym for a naïve, easily hoodwinked person.

These, however, by no means exhaust the list. "Tad" Dorgan and Hype Igoe, both of whom specialized in sporting events, began their professional careers on the San Francisco newspapers of that period, as did Gordon Ross, Reuben Goldberg, and a number of others. "Rube" Goldberg joined the staff of the *Chronicle* in 1904, at the age of twenty-one, transferred to the *Evening Bulletin* the following year, moved on to New York in 1907, and during the years that followed so amused readers from coast to coast with his syndicated "Boob McNutt" and "They'll Do It Every Time" that four decades later, in 1948, he was awarded a Pulitzer Prize.

Yet another product of the local newspaper art rooms was Harrison Fisher, a resident of Alameda across the bay, who served his apprenticeship on the *Examiner.* An excellent craftsman, his graphic portrayals of courtroom scenes, prize fights, and views of society balls and weddings enlivened the pages of that journal until Hearst called him to New York to serve in a like capacity on the *Journal.* Later Fisher became a featured illustrator for the Hearst magazines, his drawings of pretty girls appearing each month on the cover of the *Cosmopolitan* until their creator's death in 1934.

Not only the town's dailies but its weekly and monthly journals were throughout the 1890s and early 1900s valuable training schools for beginners. Among weeklies was the old-established *Wasp*, which since its founding in the early 1870s had, as stated earlier, printed in each issue a double-page colored cartoon. All these were powerfully drawn, particularly those by such staff artists as Charles Saalburg, Henry Nappenbach, and J. Landtruth. Other weeklies included the *News-Letter*, the *Golden Era*, the *Argonaut*, and the *Wave*, some of which used illustrations each week, others only in their Christmas or other special numbers.

Yet another outlet for the wares of local artists during the closing years of the century was the *Overland Monthly*. The *Overland*, which had suspended publication a few years after Bret Harte had left for the East, was revived in the mid-1880s. In its new form—which Bierce delighted to refer to as the "Warmed Overland"—illustrations were used, and so many local artists were given assignments that its editor once stated that more beginners had graduated from its columns to the New York magazines and newspapers than from any other publication in the country. By way of substantiating his boast the editor went on to list more than a score of then well-known names in that field, including not only virtually all those mentioned earlier, but Henry Raleigh, Ernest Peixotto, Arthur Cahill, Maynard Dixon, Dan Sweeney, and half a dozen others.

The town's newspapers, magazines, and lithographing shops were, however, not the only training schools available to the embryo artists of the period. As early as 1871 the San Francisco Art Association had been founded, offering day and night classes at its quarters above the California Market on

Pine Street. There, too, exhibitions of the work of students were held from time to time, in rooms that, according to one visitor, were redolent with odors arising from the stalls of the fish venders below. The association remained at that location for more than two decades, during part of which time it had as neighbors both the Bohemian Club and William Keith.

Throughout much of its earlier period the association's school was under the direction of Virgil Williams, a highly competent painter who had got his training in the ateliers of Paris and Rome. Although the school flourished, numbering among its students several who later became well known, certain members of the local art colony would have nothing to do with it. These charged that the faculty was hopelessly tradition-bound, its members ignoring the work of Manet, Degas, Monet, Cézanne, and others of the impressionists then coming to the fore in Paris.

These differences of opinion much enlivened the artistic life of the town during the next few years. One memorable hassle revolved about nineteen-year-old Henry Barkhaus, an uncommonly talented cartoonist whose drawings appeared from time to time on the middle pages of the *Wasp.* Barkhaus was one of Virgil Williams's prize students, and when Williams urged him to go to Munich and continue his studies there, certain of the youth's artist friends protested violently, arguing that the result would be to convert an extremely able cartoonist into a mediocre painter. Whether or not the experience would have had the dire result they prophesied must be left to conjecture, for not long after young Barkhaus reached the German city he fell victim to typhoid fever and died.

The Art Association remained in its Pine Street rooms until 1893, then moved up to the top of Nob Hill, taking over the big Hopkins mansion on the southeast corner of California and Mason streets. That ornate structure, built in the late

1870s by one of the railroad Big Four, Mark Hopkins—who did not live long enough to occupy it—had long been vacant. For after Hopkins's death his widow had moved East and put up a second—and even more pretentious—residence at Great Barrington, Massachusetts. There she met a young man named Edward T. Searles, an employee of a New York decorating firm that had been commissioned to furnish her Great Barrington chateau. The pair were married and, after her death in 1891, her will disclosed that she had left her entire estate to Searles. This, of course, included the long-idle San Francisco house, and locally there was much speculation as to what the new owner planned to do with the property. This uncertainty was ended, however, two years later when Searles presented it to the San Francisco Art Association.

For the next dozen years—until the building and most of its contents were consumed in the holocaust of 1906—it remained the center about which revolved much of the artistic and Bohemian life of the town. Its baroque ground-floor salons and drawing rooms were converted into exhibition galleries and classrooms, and many of the spacious chambers on the floors above were taken over as studios. Twice each year, in the spring and fall, exhibitions were held, to which all San Franciscans with any pretentions to artistic appreciation faithfully made their way. Each winter the students put on what presently came to be looked on as one of the major social events of the season, a picturesque—and seldom sedate— Mardi Gras ball, with all attending wearing colorful masquerade costumes, and the high point of which was the crowning, on the stroke of midnight, of the King and Queen of Bohemia.

III.

One student of Virgil Williams during the period before the art school moved up to Nob Hill was a twenty-one-year-old youth named Gutzon Borglum who had recently arrived from his native Idaho. Young Borglum's stay in San Francisco was comparatively brief, for in 1888—having shown unmistakable talent both as a painter and sculptor—he went on to Paris, where he studied at the Académie Julien and the Ecole des Beaux-Arts. In the early 1900s he returned to this country and during the next four decades undertook a series of progressively more important commissions, his career reaching a fitting climax with his fashioning of the heads of Washington, Jefferson, Lincoln, and Theodore Roosevelt on the cliff at Mount Rushmore, South Dakota.

Two other sculptors of the period—both far more closely identified with the city than Borglum—were Robert I. Aitken, whose local works include the Dewey Monument in Union Square, and Earl Cummings, creator of numerous statues still standing in the city's parks and squares. Both Aitken and Cummings were at one time students of an able and widely admired sculptor named Douglas Tilden. Tilden, who had been deaf since childhood, had studied under the French sculptor, Paul Chopin, himself a deaf-mute, and had returned to San Francisco in the early 1890s. Among Tilden's best-known works is the Mechanics Monument at the junction of Market, Bush, and Battery streets, a massive bronze group erected in 1899 as a memorial to Peter Donahue, pioneer mechanic and founder of the Union Iron Works.

One of the most brilliant—and tragic—figures in the artistic life of the town during the 1890s and early 1900s was the sculptor, Arthur Putnam, whose extraordinarily lifelike animals are today to be found in leading museums both in this country and abroad.

Putnam's first entry into Bohemia-by-the-Bay was in the mid-1880s, when, a callow youth in his early twenties, he appeared one day at the Art Students' League at Montgomery and Washington streets, drew from his pocket a crumpled roll of sketches of cowboys and bucking broncos—feeble imitations of the drawings of Frederic Remington—and made known his wish to enroll.

The Art Students' League, formed a few years earlier by the group of nonconformists who had broken away from the conservative Art Association, then occupied the top floor of a ramshackle building that had once housed the Brokers' Exchange and later the Probate Court. The artists had taken over the ornate, high-ceilinged courtroom, dividing it into a series of classrooms and studios by means of movable, burlap-covered screens.

The first person Putnam encountered on his initial visit chanced to be one of the instructors, Julie Heyneman, herself a portrait painter of considerable note. To her he confided that he had amassed thirty dollars while working as a ranch hand in San Diego County, and that he proposed to "study art" as long as his nest egg lasted, his aim being to get a job as staff artist on one of the local newspapers. Unimpressed by the drawings he showed her, and annoyed at his brash manner—which she later realized was his way of covering up an inherent shyness—she decided to take the bumptious youth down a peg or two. Seating him before an easel and putting a stick of charcoal in his hand, she placed before him a plaster cast of a Greek discus thrower and asked him to make a drawing of that.

She had left him no more than a minute or two when he

loudly summoned her back, announcing that his sketch was finished. That was too much for the normally placid Miss Heyneman. She returned prepared to reprove him sharply for his haste and carelessness. Her mounting anger vanished, however, when she saw what he had produced. For in a few bold strokes he had caught the strength and grace of the figure in a way that amazed her; here obviously was an embryo artist of no ordinary talent.

Putnam spent the next several weeks at the school, sleeping on a couch in the League's quarters and sweeping out the big room in return for his lodgings. One day he showed his instructress a pipe bowl he had carved from a manzanita root dug up on his father's ranch: the head and torso of a woman, its workmanship so deft and sure as to convince her that the youth's real forte was sculpture. She accordingly sent him to the nearby studio of a sculptor named Rupert Schmidt, with a note stating that its bearer showed evidences of talent and urging that he be taken on as a helper.

During the next several years Putnam worked for a number of sculptors throughout the country, among them Edward Kemeys in Chicago, whose specialty was animals. Then, having married, he and his wife returned to San Francisco and took quarters in a little hotel across Montgomery Street from the League. There throughout much of the 1890s they shared the carefree, hand-to-mouth existence of the group that lived and worked in the area. Among them were, besides Julie Heyneman, Bruce Porter, designer of stained-glass windows; architect Willis Polk, then at the beginning of an illustrious career; Henry Atkins of the art firm of Vickery, Atkins & Torrey; and, among painters, Arthur Mathews, Fred Yates, Theodore Wores, Anne Bremer, Florence Lundborg, Will Sparks, and Maynard Dixon. Putnam, by all accounts, fitted in well with that buoyant, carefree group, always high-spirited and fun-loving, and ever ready to take part in their festivities and pranks.

It was through Willis Polk and architects John Bakewell and Arthur Brown that the youth received commissions that first made the quality of his work known: exquisitely done scale models of buildings about to be built, as well as decorative friezes and other embellishments of their exteriors and lobbies.

Installed in a draughty studio on the roof of a building on Washington Street below Kearny, he presently began turning out the exquisite animal statues for which he was to become famous. But the market for such works was far from booming and the going was often hard. One visitor later recalled that a 200-pound sack of beans stood in a corner of the studio, and that Putnam once pointed it out as their only reliance when, as frequently happened, there was no money to buy other food. To help out, he took a job as teacher at the League, one of his pupils being Ralph Stackpole, who later became a sculptor of note. Occasionally he would sell one of his animal statues to local art fanciers, charging for them twenty-five dollars or less—extraordinary bargains in view of what such works were to bring a few years later.

His first big break came when his brother George, who had become secretary to E. W. Scripps, founder of the Scripps chain of newspapers, interested the publisher in his work. The young sculptor was summoned to Scripps's 2,000-acre estate at Miramar, near San Diego, and returned with a commission to do a series of statues to adorn its grounds. During the months that followed, he commuted between San Francisco and Miramar, showing his sponsor first sketches, then plaster models of the proposed works, which were planned to depict different phases of pioneer life in California. The statues, of heroic size, were to be cast in bronze, the sculptor planning to devote a full year to the production of each. Fortified by that grandiose commission, he and his wife set off for Europe, his intention being to find a studio in or near Paris and remain there until the entire job was finished.

As it turned out, none of the Scripps statues was ever made. For throughout his stay abroad the hitherto robust young man was plagued by a series of illnesses and the consequence was that at the end of a year and a half he returned to San Francisco. During his sojourn in Paris he had, however, fashioned and cast in bronze a number of statues of California animals—bears, pumas, jaguars, deer, coyotes, and others—and these, on being exhibited there and later in London and New York, first heralded to the art world the arrival of a highly gifted new sculptor.

Sales, however, were still few and far between, and the next several years saw a repetition of the hand-to-mouth life he had known during his earlier stay. This time, instead of returning to the Bohemian quarter downtown, he put up a rough-board studio in the sandhills far out toward the ocean, and there he was presently spending long hours in what one friend termed a "fury of work." For the 1906 fire had meantime occurred and, rebuilding having got promptly under way, he soon found himself deluged with work. Much of this he did in his studio out near the beach. For the larger pieces, however, mainly architectural ornaments for downtown office structures, he rented two barnlike buildings at the edge of the burned area, one on Sacramento Street just west of Van Ness Avenue, the other on Divisadero Street.

The amount of work he did during that period was, by any standard, extraordinary. For in addition to his animal bronzes and his architectural designs, he was still busy perfecting his models for the huge Scripps statues. Some idea of the diversity of his work at that time may be gained from two examples still to be seen on San Francisco streets: plaster bas-reliefs of nymphs and satyrs at the entrance to one of the Pacific Street dance halls, and the design of pioneer scenes and prowling pumas on the base of the trolley poles throughout the downtown area.

That period of working long hours under high pressure was destined to have a disastrous result. He presently fell ill and, his malady having been diagnosed as brain tumor, an immediate operation was decided on. This was successful in so far as the patient survived, but it would have been less tragic had the outcome been fatal. For the injury to his brain was such that on his physical recovery it was found that his creative skill and his capacity for self-criticism had completely deserted him. He moved to Paris in 1922 and died there eight years later, still futilely trying to regain some measure of his old mastery.

IV.

April 18, 1906, marked an all-important turning point in San Francisco's annals, the sudden, violent close of one phase of the city's evolution and the opening of a new. During the half century which has passed since that catastrophe, the old-time residents—their number growing fewer year by year—have looked back with nostalgia on the prefire town, painting its attractions in colors a little too bright to be quite real and extending their sympathy to those who know only the big, bustling, materialistic city that has sprung up in its place.

While there is ample evidence that the rose-tinted memories of these ancients present a romanticized picture of the city that was, yet there can be little doubt that all through the 1890s and into the early years of the new century those who were by nature attuned to its environment found it an uncommonly stimulating place to live. This is borne out by the fact that, as these pages may in part have made clear, the earlier town extended a gracious welcome to workers in the arts, and in whatever fields their interests chanced to lay, whether in painting, writing, music, the drama, or those less esoteric fields—including food and drink and the cultivation of leisure—that make for pleasant, civilized living.

And never was the buoyant spirit of the residents more clearly demonstrated than by their behavior during the tragic period when their city was visited, first by an earthquake of unprecedented violence, then by fires that raged unchecked for three days, reducing to rubble its entire central area. The manner in which they met that crisis aroused the admiration of the entire nation. For with every building in a district comprising more than 500 blocks destroyed, and more than 250,-000 rendered homeless, the morale of the vast majority of the people remained high. Little time was wasted in futile repining; huddled in hastily thrown up refugee camps beyond the burned area, they were far too busy laying plans for rebuilding their town on a grander, more imposing scale.

It was a period when every scrap of humor that tended to brighten the grim picture was treasured. While the ruins were still smoking, copies of a New York newspaper arrived containing an editorial gravely speculating on whether or not the site would be permanently abandoned; these were passed from hand to hand and read to tatters, rarely failing to bring forth a lusty laugh. Gertrude Atherton interviewed the venerable scientist George Davidson at his house on Washington Street, a few blocks beyond the burned area, and inquired as to the intensity of the quake. Davidson replied that seismologically it would be rated as No. 9—No. 10 being complete destruction—then amused the populace by adding: "But I think A-1 would be a far better name for it!"

Even the town's poets presently joined in the fun, one local wit, Larry Harris, saluting the devastated downtown area with his *The Damnedest Finest Ruins*. Even more widely quoted was a quatrain by Charles K. Field. Having noted that by one of the quirks of the fire a few buildings in the vicinity of Montgomery and Washington streets—including one housing the Hotaling distillery—had escaped destruction, he produced the following:

> If, as they say, God spanked the town
> For being over-frisky—
> Why did He burn the churches down
> And spare Hotaling's whisky?

Repeated, too, were countless little dramas that took place during those hectic three days, particularly if they had a humorous slant. Here is one that made the rounds, and on which we might fittingly close. Following the first violent shocks on the morning of the eighteenth, Mrs. Kate Kimball, an elderly widow, dressed hastily and made her way to the street from her room on the side of Nob Hill just above Chinatown. For the next several hours she stood with the crowd on the sidewalk watching a half dozen fires mushroom over the flats below. Presently a squad of soldiers, rifles in hand, came up the hill, ordering all to move on westward, for that part of the city was doomed.

Mrs. Kimball joined the retreating throng, but she had gone only a few yards when a thought occurred to her that caused her to rush back into the house and up to her room. Her late husband's picture! She reappeared a few seconds later clutching a big framed portrait under her arm and joined the fleeing crowd. Some ten minutes later, on the rise of the hill beyond Van Ness Avenue, a prosperous-appearing man who had been watching the passing refugees singled out the old lady and addressed her, asking if she had managed to save any of her belongings.

"Only this," returned she, holding up the picture. "Only this likeness of my dear, dead husband."

At sight of the portrait the other became both solicitous and deferential. Taking her gently by the arm, he led her to his carriage nearby, drove her to his residence farther out in the Western Addition, and installed her in a spacious bedroom, telling her she must consider herself an honored guest of the household as long as she wished to stay.

It was not until her host had withdrawn that the puzzled woman learned what had prompted his extraordinary hospitality. For, on placing her treasured picture on the mantel, she discovered that in her haste and excitement she had seized a portrait not of the late Mr. Kimball, but of Ulysses S. Grant.

INDEX

Aitken, Robert I., 73, 102, 103, 232
Alcazar Theater, 118
Allan Quartermain, 142
Anderson, Mary, 77, 117
Andrews, "Colonel," 79–80
Appeal (Carson City), 155
Argonaut, 132–33, 137, 172, 202, 203, 229
Art Students' League, 233
Astronomical Society, 69
Atelier Julian, 198
Atherton, Faxon, 201
Atherton, George, 201
Atherton, Gertrude, 28, 133, 154, 201–5, 238
Atkins, Henry, 234
Auctioneer, The, 119
Austin, Mary, 176, 177

Bacon, Frank, 118
Bakewell, John, 235
Baldwin, E. J. ("Lucky"), 77, 78
Baldwin Hotel, 77, 78
Baldwin Theater, 77, 78
Bamford, Frederick I., 193, 195
Bancroft, Hubert Howe, 161–65
Bank Exchange, 59–60, 107, 182
Barbary Coast, 18–21, 92

Barkhaus, Henry, 230
Barrett, Lawrence, 116
Barrymore, Maurice, 77
Bates, Blanche, 118
Battle of Mussel Slough, 145
Beach, Chilion, 156, 202
Belasco, David, 78, 119
Benét, William Rose, 179
Bierce, Albert, 185
Bierce, Ambrose, 72, 131, 132, 137, 179–80, 184–90, 204–5, 208, 213, 229
Bigelow, Harry ("Petey"), 148–51, 200
Blix, 97–99, 199, 200
Bohemian Club, 72, 74, 83, 186, 207, 230
Bolton, Judge John H., 62
Bonner, Geraldine, 133
Booth, Edwin, 117
Borglum, Gutzon, 232
Bosqui, Edward, 157
Brady, William A., 116
Brannan, Sam, 174
Bremer, Anne, 179, 234
Britt, Jimmy, 29
Bromley, George, 72
Brooklyn Alley, 21
Brooklyn Hotel, 94
Brown, Arthur, 235

244